PATANJALI YOGA SUTRAS

TRANSLATED WITH A NEW COMMENTARY

BY SWAMI PRABHAVANANDA

AND CHRISTOPHER ISHERWOOD

Sri Ramakrishna Math

MYLAPORE MADRAS 600 004

Published by
The President
Sri Ramakrishna Math
Mylapore, Chennai-4

XIV-3M 3C-8-2005
ISBN 81-7823-108-5

Export of this book outside India is expressly prohibited.

Printed in India at
Sri Ramakrishna Math Printing Press
Mylapore, Chennai-4

PUBLISHER'S NOTE

It is with great pleasure that we present to our readers the Indian Edition of 'How to know God' * by Swami Prabhavananda.

This English translation of Patanjali's Yoga Sutras was originally published by the Vedanta Society, Southern California for the benefit of Western readers who do not know Sanskrit and yet are interested in Indian psychology which plumbs the depths of the human mind. Swami Prabhavananda who has to his credit such lucid expositions as 'Srimad Bhagavad Gita, the wisdom of God', 'Narada's way of Divine Love' and the 'Sermon on the Mount according to Vedanta' has taken special pains in this book to present the philosophy and practice of Yoga in a non-technical, up-to-date phraseology that can be understood and enjoyed by all enquiring minds. For the benefit of our Indian readers we have added also the text of Patanjali's Sutras in Devanagari.

We are sure that they will find the book eminently helpful in their spiritual practice. We are thankful to Swami Prabhavanandaji and the Vedanta Society, Southern California for kind permission to bring out this Indian edition.

Sri Ramakrishna Math PUBLISHER
Madras 600 004

---

* Now the book is titled *Patanjali Yoga Sutras*

CONTENTS

TRANSLATORS' FOREWORD

Patanjali's Yoga Sutras (Aphorisms) are not the original exposition of a philosophy, but a work of compilation and reformulation. References to yoga practices—spiritual disciplines and techniques of meditation which enable a man to achieve unitive knowledge of the Godhead—are to be found, already, in the Katha, Svetasvatara, Taittiriya, and Maitrayani Upanishads, very many centuries earlier. Indeed, the yoga doctrine may be said to have been handed down from pre-historic times.

What Patanjali did was to restate yoga philosophy and practice for the man of his own period. But what *was* his period? And who was Patanjali? Hardly anything is known about him. Some authorities believe that there were actually two Patanjalis, one a grammarian and the other the author of the Sutras. Others deny this. As for the date of the Sutras, the guesses of scholars vary widely, ranging from the fourth century B.C. to the fourth century A.D.

The simplest meaning of the word sutra is "thread". A sutra is, so to speak, the bare thread of an exposition, the absolute minimum that is necessary to hold it together, unadorned by a single "bead" of elaboration. Only essential words are used. Often, there is no complete sentence-structure. There was a good reason for this method. Sutras were composed at a period when there were no books. The entire work had to be memorized, and so it had to be expressed as tersely as possible. Patanjali's Sutras, like all others, were intended to be expanded and explained. The ancient teachers would repeat an aphorism by heart and then proceed to amplify it with their own comments, for the benefit of their pupils. In some instances these comments, also, were memorized, transcribed at a later date, and thus preserved for us.

In this translation we have not only provided a commentary but expanded and paraphrased the aphorisms themselves, so that each one becomes an intelligible statement in the English language. Certain other translators have been unwilling to take this liberty, and have therefore offered a version of the text which is approximately literal, but as cryptic as a professor's lecture notes. It cannot be understood at all until its commentary has been carefully studied. We believe that this kind of translation has a bad psychological effect on the reader. Being, at first glance, unable to make anything of the aphorisms themselves, he is apt to decide that the whole subject is too difficult for him. Enough difficulties exist anyway in the study of yoga philosophy. It has been our aim not to increase them unnecessarily.

Our commentary is mainly our own work. However, we have followed the explanations of the two ancient commentators, Bhoja and Vyasa. We have also quoted frequently from the brilliant and deeply intuitive comments of Swami Vivekananda. These comments were made extempore during the classes on Patanjali which the Swami held in the United States more than fifty years ago. They were written down by his students, and are included in his book on *Raja Yoga.*

Since yoga, prior to Patanjali, was originally grounded in Vedanta philosophy, we have interrupted the aphorisms, throughout, from a Vedantist viewpoint. In this we differ from Patanjali himself, who was a follower of Sankhya philosophy. But these are merely technical differences, and it is best not to insist on them too strongly, lest the reader become confused. They are breifly explained at appropriate points in our country.

In general, we have wished to present in this book as a practical aid to the spiritual life; an aid that can used by the devotees of any religion—Hindu, Christian, or other. We have therefore avoided dwelling much on its metaphysical and occult aspects. The study of these may fascinate some types of mind, but it is ultimately sterile and may even be dangerous if carried to excess.

It was suggested to us, while we were working on the book, that we should introduce into it a comparison of yoga and modern Western psychology. Such a comparison has already been attempted by various writers, and some interesting points of similarity and dissimilarity in theory and technique have been noted. But, from our view at least, the comparison in itself seems neither fair nor valid. Yoga psychology is a finished product. Western psychology is still developing and along several divergent lines; continually producing new theories and discarding old ones. If one says categorically: "Western psychology hold this view....," one is always in danger of being reprimanded for inaccuracy.

We may, however, make one statement safely. The majority of Western psychotherapists do not, as yet, recognize the existence of the Atman, the Godhead within man; and do not therefore, attempt to help their patients achieve the union of perfect yoga. As for those psychotherapists, now becoming quite numerous, who take a serious interest in yoga, many of them would no doubt state their position somewhat as follows: "We can help our patients to a certain point—to an adequate degree of adjustment on the psychological level. Beyond that, we're not ready to go. We recognize the possibility of a higher, spiritual integration, but we prefer not to make it a part of our therapy, because we believe that the two should be kept separate. If a patient wants spiritual integration, we can only send him to a yoga teacher or a minister of religion. Where we leave off, yoga begins."

And there, for the present, the problem rests.

In conclusion, we must gratefully acknowledge the permission given us to quote from the following books. Erwin Schrodinger's *What is Life*? published by the Cambridge University Press; the volume containing *The Way of a Pilgrim* and *The Pilgrim Continues His Way,* translated by R.M. French and published by the Society for Promoting Christian Knowledge, of London; the Bhagavad Gita, translated by the present authors and published by New American Library, and the following works published by the Vedanta Press of Hollywood: Shankara's *Crest-Jewel of Discrimination* (Prabhavananda-Isherwood), *The Eternal Companion* Prabhavananda), and the Upanishads (Prabhavananda–Manchester).

I. YOGA AND ITS AIMS

अथ योगानुशासनम् ॥ १ ॥

1. This is the beginning of instruction in yoga.

Basically, *yoga* means "*union.*" It is the Sanskrit ancestor of the English word "yoke." Hence, it comes to mean a method of spiritual union. A yoga is a method—any one of many—by which an individual may become united with the Godhead, the Reality which underlies this apparent, ephemeral universe. To achieve such union is to reach the state of perfect yoga. Christianity has a corresponding term, "the mystic union," which expresses a similar idea.

Bhoja, one of the classical commentators on these aphorisms, defines Patanjali's use of the word yoga as "an effort to separate the Atman (the Reality) from the non-Atman (the apparent)."

One who practises yoga is called a yogi.

योगश्चित्तवृत्तिनिरोधः ॥ २ ॥

2. Yoga is the control of thought-waves in the mind.

According to Patanjali, the mind (*chitta*) is made up of three components, *manas*, *buddhi*, and *ahamkara*. Manas is the recording faculty which receives impressions gathered by the senses from the outside world. Buddhi is the discriminative faculty which classifies these impressions and reacts to them. Ahamkara is the ego-sense which claims these impressions for its own and stores them up as individual knowledge. For example, manas reports: "A large animate object is quickly approaching." Buddhi decides: "That's a bull. It is angry. It wants to attack someone." Ahamkara screams: "It wants to attack *me*, Patanjali. It is *I* who see this bull. It is *I* who am frightened. It is *I* who am about to run away." Later, from the branches of a nearby tree, ahamkara may add: "Now *I* know that this bull (which is not *I*) is dangerous. There are others who do not know this; it is *my* own personal knowledge, which will cause *me* to avoid this bull in future."

God, the underlying Reality, is by definition omnipresent. If the Reality exists at all, it must be everwhere; it must be present within every sentient being, every inanimate object God-within-the-creature is known in the Sanskrit language as the *Atman* or *Purusha*, the real Self. Patanjali speaks always of the Purusha (which means literally "the Godhead that dwells within the body"), but we shall substitute Atman throughout this translation, because Atman is the word used in the Upanishads and the Bhagavad Gita, and students are therefore likely to be more accustomed to it. According to the Upanishads and the Gita, the one Atman is present within all creàtures. Patanjali, following Sankhya philosophy, believed that each individual creature and object has its separate, but identical, Purusha. This philosophical point of difference has no practical importance for the spiritual aspirant.

The mind seems to be intelligent and conscious. Yoga philosophy teaches that it is not. It has only a borrowed intelligence. The Atman is intelligence itself, is pure consciousness. The mind merely reflects that consciousness and so appears to be conscious.

Knowledge or perception is a thought-wave (*vritti*) in the mind. All knowledge is therefore objective. Even what Western psychologists call introspection or self-knowledge is objective knowledge according to Patanjali, since the mind is not the seer, but only an instrument of knowledge, an object of perception like the outside world. The Atman, the real seer, remains unknown.

Every perception arouses the ego-sense, which says: "I know this," But this is the ego speaking, not the Atman, the real Self. The ego-sense is caused by the identification of the Atman with the mind, senses etc. It is as if a little electric light bulb would declare: "I am the electric current" and then proceed to describe electricity as a pear-shaped glass object containing filaments of wire. Such identification is absurd—as absurd as the ego's claim to be the real Self. Nevertheless, the electric current is present in the light bulb, and the Atman is in all things, everywhere.

When an event or object in the external world is recorded by the senses, a thought-wave is raised in the mind. The ego-sense identifies itself with this wave. If the thought-wave is pleasant, the ego-sense feels, "I am happy"; if the wave is unpleasant, "I am unhappy." This false identification is the cause of all our misery—for even the ego's temporary sensation of happiness brings anxiety, a desire to cling to the object of pleasure, and this prepares future possibilities of becoming unhappy. The real Self, the Atman, remains forever outside the power of thought-waves; it is eternally pure, enlightened and free—the only true, unchanging happiness. It follows, therefore, that man can never know his real Self as long as the thought-waves and the ego-sense are being identified. In order to become enlightened we must bring the thought-waves under control, so that this false identification may cease. The Gita teaches us that "Yoga is the breaking of contact with pain."

Describing the action of the thought-waves, the commentators employ a simple image—the image of a lake. If the surface of a lake is lashed into waves, the water becomes muddy and the bottom cannot be seen. The lake represents the mind and the bottom of the lake the Atman.

When Patanjali speaks of "control of thought-waves," he does not refer to a momentary or superficial control. Many people believe that the practice of yoga is concerned with "making your mind a blank" — a condition which could, if it were really desirable, be much more easily achieved by asking a friend to hit you over the head with a hammer. No spiritual advantage is ever gained by self-violence. We are not trying to check the thought-waves by smashing the organs which record them. We have to do something much more difficult—to unlearn the false identification of the thought-waves with the ego-sense. This process of unlearning involves a complete transformation of character, a "renewal of the mind," as St. Paul puts it.

What does yoga philosophy mean by "character"? To explain this, one may develop the analogy of the lake. Waves do not merely disturb the surface of the water, they also, by their continued action, build up banks of sand or pebbles on the lake bottom. Such sand-banks are, of course, much more permanent and solid than the waves themselves. They may be compared to the tendencies, potentialities and latent states which exist in the subconscious and unconscious areas of the mind. In Sanskrit, they are called *samskaras.* The samskaras are built up by the continued action of the thought-waves, and they, in their turn, create new thought waves—the process works both ways. Expose the mind to constant thoughts of anger and resentment, and you will find that these anger-waves build up anger-throughout your daily life. A man with well-developed anger-samskaras is said to have "a bad temper." The sum total of our samskaras is, in fact, our character—at any given moment. Let us never forget, however, that, just as a sandbank may shift and change its shape if the tide or the current changes, so also the samskaras may be modified by the introduction of other kinds of thought-waves into the mind.

While we are on this subject it is worth referring to a difference of interpretation which exists between yoga and Western science. Not all samskaras are acquired during the course of a single human life. A child is born with certain tendencies already present in its nature. Western science is inclined to ascribe such tendencies to heredity. Yoga psychology explains that they were acquired in former incarnations, as the result of thoughts and actions long since forgotten. It does not really matter, for practical purposes, which of these two theories one prefers. "Heredity," from the yoga view-point, may be only another way of saying that the individual soul is driven by existing samskaras to seek rebirth in a certain kind of family, of parents whose samskaras are like its own, and thereby to "inherit" the tendencies which it already possesses. The yoga aspirant does not waste his time wondering where his samskaras came from or how long he has had them; he accepts full responsibility for them and sets about trying to change them.

There are, of course, many types of mind which are not yet ready for the higher yoga practices. If you have a flabby, neglected physique and try to take part in a class for ballet dancers, you will probably do yourself a great injury; you have to start with a few simple exercises. There are minds which may be described as "scattered"; they are restless, passionate and unable to concentrate. There are lazy, inert minds, incapable of constructive thought. There are also minds which, though they possess a certain degree of energy, can only dwell on what is pleasant; they shrink away from the disagreeable aspects of life. But every mind, no matter what its present nature, can ultimately be disciplined and transformed-can become, in Patanjali's phrase, "one-pointed" and fit to attain the state of perfect yoga.

तदा द्रष्टुः स्वरूपेऽवस्थानम् ॥ ३ ॥

3. Then man abides in his real nature.

When the lake of the mind becomes clear and still, man knows himself as he really is, always was and always will be. He knows that he is the Atman. His "personality," his mistaken belief in himself as a separate, unique individual, disappears. "Patanjali" is only an outer covering, like a coat or a mask, which he can assume or lay aside as he chooses. Such a man is known as a free, illumined soul.

वृत्तिसारूप्यमितरत्र ॥ ४ ॥

4. At other times, when he is not in the state of yoga, man remains identified with the thought-waves in the mind.

वृत्तयः पञ्चतय्यः क्लिष्टाऽक्लिष्टाः ॥ ५ ॥

5. There are five kinds of thought-waves — some painful, others not painful.

A "painful" wave, according to Patanjali's use of the term, is not necessarily a wave which *seems* painful when it first arises in the mind; it is a wave which brings with it an increased degree of ignorance, addiction and bondage. Similarly, a wave which seems painful at first may actually belong to the category of those which are "not painful", provided that it impels the mind toward greater freedom and knowledge. For example, Patanjali would describe a lustful thought-wave as "painful", because lust, even when pleasantly satisfied, causes addiction, jealousy and bondage to the person desired. A wave of pity, on the other hand, would be described as "not painful", because pity is an unselfish emotion which loosens the bonds of our own egotism. We may suffer deeply when we see others suffering, but our pity will teach us understanding and, hence, freedom.

This distinction between the two kinds of thought-waves is very important when we come to the actual practice of yoga discipline. For the thought-waves cannot all be controlled at once. First, we have to overcome the "painful" thought-waves by raising waves which are "not painful." To our thoughts of anger, desire and delusion we must oppose thoughts of love, generosity and truth. Only much later, when the "painful" thought-waves have been completely stilled, can we proceed to the second stage of discipline; the stilling of the "not painful" waves which we have deliberately created.

The idea that we should ultimately have to overcome even those thought-waves which are "good", "pure" and "truthful" may at first seem shocking to a student who has been trained in the Western approach to morality. But a little reflection will show him that this must be so. The external world, even in its most beautiful appearances and noblest manifestations, is still superficial and transient. It is not the basic Reality. We must look through it, not at it in order to see the Atman. Certainly, it is better to love than to hate, better to share than to hoard, better to tell the truth than to lie. But the thought-waves which motivate the practice of these virtues are nevertheless disturbances in the mind. We all know instances of admirable, earnest men who become so deeply involved in the cares of a great reform movement or social relief project that they cannot think of anything beyond the practical problems of their daily work. Their minds are not calm. They are full of anxiety and restlessness. The mind of the truly illumined man is calm—not because he is selfishly indifferent to the needs of others, but because he knows the peace of the Atman within all things, even within the appearance of misery, disease, strife and want.

प्रमाण - विपर्यय - विकल्प - निद्रा - स्मृतयः ॥ ६ ॥

6. These five kinds of thought-waves are: right knowledge, wrong knowledge, verbal delusion, sleep and memory.

प्रत्यक्षानुमानागमाः प्रमाणानि ॥ ७ ॥

7. The right kinds of knowledge are: direct perception, inference and scriptural testimony.

Whatever our senses preceive is right knowledge, provided that there has been no element of delusion. Whatever we infer from our direct perception is also right knowledge, provided that our reasoning is correct. The scriptures are based upon the superconscious knowledge obtained by great spiritual teachers while in the state of perfect yoga. Therefore they also are right knowledge. They represent a kind of direct perception far more immediate than the perceptions of the senses, and the truths they teach can be verified by anyone who attains to this superconscious vision.

विपर्ययो मिथ्याज्ञानमतद्रूपप्रतिष्ठम् ॥ ८ ॥

8. Wrong knowledge is knowledge which is false and not based upon the true nature of its object.

The classic example given in yoga literature is that of a piece of rope which is mistaken for a snake. In this case, wrong knowledge will cause us to fear the rope and avoid it or try to kill it.

शब्दज्ञानानुपाती वस्तुशून्यो विकल्पः ॥ ९ ॥

9. Verbal delusion arises when words do not correspond to reality.

A common form of verbal delusion is jumping to conclusions. We hear somebody speaking and form a hasty and inaccurate picture of his meaning. In political speeches one often finds a *double* verbal delusion: the speaker believes that his words correspond to one reality, the audience attaches them to another—and both are wrong. Such expressions as "the spirit of democracy", "the American way of life", and so forth, bear rich crops of verbal delusion every year, in the newspapers and over the radio.

अभाव-प्रत्ययालम्बना वृत्तिर्निद्रा ॥ १० ॥

10. Sleep is a wave of thought about nothingness.

That is to say, dreamless sleep is not an absence of thought-waves in the mind, but a positive experience of nothingness. It cannot therefore be confused with the waveless state of yoga. If there were no thought-waves in the mind during sleep, we should not wake remembering that we knew nothing. As S. Radhakrishnan remarks in his *Philosophy*, Mr. So-and-So, after a good sleep, goes on being Mr. So-and-So, since his experiences unite themselves to the system which existed at the time when he went to sleep. They link themselves to his thoughts and do not fly to any other's. Such continuity of experience makes it necessary for us to admit a permanent Self underlying all contents of consciousness.

अनुभूतविषयासम्प्रमोषः स्मृतिः ॥ ११ ॥

11. Memory is when perceived objects are not forgotten, but come back to consciousness.

Memory is a kind of secondary thought-wave. A wave of direct perception causes a smaller ripple or series of ripples. The thought-wave of sleep also causes smaller ripples, which we call dreams. Dreaming is remembering in your sleep

अभ्यासवैराग्याभ्यां तन्निरोधः ॥ १२ ॥

12. They are controlled by means of practice and non-attachment.

तत्र स्थितौ यत्नोऽभ्यासः ॥ १३ ॥

13. Practice is the repeated effort to follow the disciplines which give permanent control of the thought-waves of the mind.

स तु दीर्घकालनैरन्तर्यसत्कारासेवितो दृढभूमिः ॥ १४ ॥

14. Practice becomes firmly grounded when it has been cultivated for a long time, uninterruptedly, with earnest devotion.

दृष्टानुश्रविकविषयवितृष्णस्य वशीकारसंज्ञा वैराग्यम् ॥ १५ ॥

15. Non-attachment is self-mastery; it is freedom from desire for what is seen or heard.

The waves of the mind can be made to flow in two opposite directions—either toward the objective world ("the will to desire") or toward true self-knowledge ("the will to liberation"). Therefore both practice and non-attachment are necessary. Indeed, it is useless and even dangerous to attempt one without the other. If we try to practice spiritual disciplines without attempting to control the thought-waves of desire, our minds will become violently agitated and perhaps permanently unbalanced. If we attempt nothing more than a rigid negative control of the waves of desire, without raising waves of love, compassion and devotion to oppose them, then the result may be even more tragic. This is why certain strict puritans suddenly and mysteriously commit suicide. They make a cold, stern effort to be "good"—that is, not to think "bad" thoughts—and when they fail, as all human beings sometimes must, they cannot face this humiliation, which is really nothing but hurt pride, and the emptiness inside themselves. In the Taoist scriptures we read: "Heaven arms with compassion those whom it would not see destroyed"

The spiritual disciplines which we are to practice will be described in due course. They are known as the eight "limbs" of yoga. Perseverance is very important, in this connection. No temporary failure, however disgraceful or humiliating, should ever be used as an excuse for giving up the struggle. If we are learning to ski, we are not ashamed when we fall down, or find ourselves lying in some ridiculous entangled position. We pick ourselves up and start again. Never mind if people laugh, or sneer at us. Unless we are hypocrites we shall not care what impression we make upon the onlookers. No failure is ever really a failure unless we stop trying altogether—indeed, it may be a blessing in disguise, a much-needed lesson.

Non-attachment is the exercise of discrimination. We gradually gain control of the "painful" or impure thought-waves by asking ourselves: "Why do I really desire that object? What permanent advantage should I gain by possessing it? In what way would its possession help me toward greater knowledge and freedom?" The answers to these questions are always disconcerting. They show us that the desired object is not only useless as a means to liberation but potentially harmful as a means to ignorance and bondage; and, further, that our desire is not really desire for the object-in-itself at all, but only a desire to desire something, a mere restlessness in the mind.

It is fairly easy to reason all this out in a calm moment. But our non-attachment is put to the test when the mind is suddenly swept by a huge wave of anger or lust or greed. Then it is only by a determined effort of will that we can remember what our reason already knows—that this wave, and the sense-object which raised it, and the ego-sense which identifies the experience with itself, are all alike transient and superficial—that they are not the underlying Reality.

Non-attachment may come very slowly. But even its earliest stages are rewarded by a new sense of freedom and peace. It should never be thought of as an austerity, a kind of self-torture, something grim and painful. The practice of non-attachment gives value and significance to even the most ordinary incidents of the dullest day. It eliminates boredom from our lives. And, as we progress and gain increasing self-mastery, we shall see that we are renouncing nothing that we really need or want, we are only freeing ourselves from imaginary needs and desires. In this spirit, a soul grows in greatness until it can accept life's worst disasters, calm and unmoved. Christ said, "For, my yoke is easy and my burden is light" —meaning that the ordinary undiscriminating life of sense-attachment is really much more painful, much harder to bear, than the disciplines which will set us free. We find this saying difficult to understand because we have been trained to think of Christ's earthly life as tragic—a glorious, inspiring tragedy, certainly—but ending nevertheless upon a cross. We should rather ask ourselves: "Which would be easier—to hang on that cross with the enlightenment and non-attachment of a Christ, or to suffer there in the ignorance and agony and bondage of a poor thief?" And the cross may come to us anyway, whether we are ready and able to accept it or not.

तत्परं पुरुषख्यातेर्गुणवैतृष्ण्यम् ॥ १६ ॥

16. When, through knowledge of the Atman, one ceases to desire any manifestation of Nature, then that is the highest kind of non-attachment.

Non-attachment is *not* indifference—this cannot be repeated too often. Many people reject the aims of yoga philosophy as "inhuman" and "selfish", because they imagine yoga as a cold, deliberate shunning of everybody and everything for the sake of working out one's own salvation. The truth is exactly opposite. Human love is the highest emotion most of us know. It frees us to some extent from our egotism in our relation to one or more individuals. But human love is still possessive and exclusive. Love for the Atman is neither. We readily admit that it is better to love people "for what they really are" than merely for their beauty, their intelligence, their strength, their sense of humour or some other quality—but this is only a vague and relative phrase. What people "really are" is the Atman, nothing less. To love the Atman in ourselves is to love it everywhere. And to love the Atman everywhere is to go beyond any manifestation of Nature to the Reality within Nature. Such a love is too vast to be understood by ordinary minds, and yet it is simply an infinite deepening and expansion of the little limited love we all experience. To love someone, even in the usual human manner, is to get a brief, dim glimpse of something within that person which is tremendous, awe-inspiring, and eternal. In our ignorance, we think that this "something" is unique. He or she, we say, is like nobody else. That is because our perception of the Reality is clouded and obscured by the external manifestations—the character and individual qualities of the person we love—and by the way in which our own ego-sense reacts to them. Nevertheless, this weak flash of perception is a valid spiritual experience and it should encourage us to purify our minds and make them fit for that infinitely greater kind of love which always awaits us. This love is not restless or transient, like our human love. It is secure and eternal and calm. It is absolutely free from desire, because lover and beloved have become one.

Note the following from the Bhagavad Gita:

> Water flows continually into the ocean
> But the ocean is never disturbed:
> Desire flows into the mind of the seer
> But he is never disturbed.
> The seer knows peace...
> He knows peace who has forgotten desire.
> He lives without craving:
> Free from ego, free from pride.

वितर्कविचारानन्दास्मितानुगमात् सम्प्रज्ञातः ॥ १७ ॥

17. Concentration upon a single object may reach four stages: examination, discrimination, joyful peace and simple awareness of individuality.

In order to understand this and the following aphorisms, we must now study the structure of the universe as it is presented in *Vedanta* philosophy. (Vedanta is the philosophy based on the teachings of the Vedas— the earliest Hindu scriptures). First let us consider the basic Reality. The Reality considered as the innermost Self of any particular creature or object, is called the Atman—as we have already seen. When the Reality is spoken of in its universal aspect, it is called *Brahman.* This may sound confusing, at first, to Western students, but the concept should not be strange to them. Christian terminology employs two phrases—God immanent and God transcendent—which make a similar distinction. Again and again, in Hindu and Christian literature, we find this great paradox restated—that God is both within and without, instantly present and infinitely elsewhere, the dweller in the atom and the abode of all things. But this is the same Reality, the same Godhead, seen in its two relations to the cosmos. These relations are described by two different words simply in order to help us think about them. They imply no kind of duality. Atman and Brahman are one.

What is this cosmos? What is it made of? Vedanta teaches that the cosmos is made of *Prakriti,* the elemental, undifferentiated stuff of mind and matter. Prakriti is defined as the power or effect of Brahman—in the sense that heat is a power or effect of fire. Just as heat cannot exist apart from the fire which causes it, so Prakriti could not exist apart from Brahman. The two are eternally inseparable. The latter puts forth and causes the former.

Patanjali differed from Vedanta on this point, believing that the Purusha (or Atman) and Prakriti were two separate entities, both equally real and eternal. Since, however, Patanjali also believed that the individual Purusha could be entirely liberated and isolated from Prakriti, he was, in fact, in complete agreement with Vedanta as to the aim and goal of spiritual life.

Why does Brahman cause Prakriti? This is a question which cannot possibly be answered in the terms of any man-made philosophy. For the human intellect is itself within Prakriti and therefore cannot comprehend its nature. A great seer may experience the nature of the Brahman-Prakriti relationship while he is in the state of perfect yoga, but he cannot communicate his knowledge to us in terms of logic and language because, from an absolute standpoint, Prakriti does not exist. It is not the Reality—and yet it is not other than the Reality. It is the Reality as it seems to our human senses—the Reality distorted, limited, misread. We may accept, as a working hypothesis, the seer's assurance that this is so, but our intellects reel away, baffled, from the tremendous mystery. Lacking superconscious experience, we have to be content with picture-talk. We come back gratefully to Shelley's famous lines:

> Life, like a dome of many-coloured glass,
> Stains the white radiance of eternity.

Philosophically, they may be rather vague—it is not clear exactly what Shelly means by "Life"—but they do provide us with a useful and beautiful image: if we think of Brahman as "the white radiance", then Prakriti is represented by the colours which disguise the real nature of its beams.

Prakriti, it has been said, is the elemental undifferentiated stuff of mind and matter. In what relation does it stand to the highly differentiated phenomena of this apparent universe? In order to answer this question, we must trace the whole course of a creation from the beginning. We say "a creation" deliberately—for Hindu philosophy sees creation and dissolution as an endlessly repeated process. When, from time to time, the universe dissolves—or apparently dissolves—it is said to go back into undifferentiated Prakriti and to remain there, in a potential "seed-state", for a certain period. What, then, is the mechanism of its re-creation? Prakriti is said to be composed of three forces, *sattwa*, *rajas* and *tamas*, which are known collectively as the three *gunas*. These gunas—whose individual characteristics we shall describe in a moment—pass through phases of equilibrium and phases of imbalance; the nature of their relationship to each other is such that it is subject to perpetual change. As long as the gunas maintain their equilibrium, Prakriti remains undifferentiated and the universe exists only in its potential state. As soon as the balance is disturbed, a re-creation of the universe begins. The gunas enter into an enormous variety of combinations—all of them irregular, with one or the other guna predominating over the rest. Hence we have the variety of physical and psychic phenomena which make up our apparent world. Such a world continues to multiply and vary its forms until the gunas find a temporary equilibrium once more, and a new phase of undifferentiated potentiality begins. (A scientifically minded student should compare Vedanta cosmology with the latest theories of atomic physics. He will find many points of resemblance between the two systems.)

The gunas are sometimes described as "energies," sometimes as "qualities"; but no single English word can define their whole nature and function. Collectively, they may be thought of as a triangle of forces, opposed yet complementary. In the process of evolution, sattwa is the essence of the form which has to be realized, tamas is the inherent obstacle to its realization, and rajas is the power by which that obstacle is removed and the essential form made manifest. For the sake of illustration, let us take a human rather than a cosmic example. A sculptor decides to make a figure of a horse. The idea of this horse—the form of it which he sees in his imagination—is inspired by sattwa. Now he gets a lump of clay. This clay represents the power of tamas—its formlessness is an obstacle which has to be overcome. Perhaps, also, there is an element of tamas in the sculptor's own mind. He may think: "This is going to be a lot of trouble. It's too difficult. I'm tired. Why should I make the effort?" But here the force of rajas comes to his aid. Rajas, in this instance, represents the sculptor's will to conquer his own lethargy and the difficulties of his medium; it represents, also, the muscular exertion which he puts forth in order to complete his work. If a sufficient amount of rajas is generated, the obstacle of tamas will be overcome and the ideal form of sattwa will be embodied in a tangible clay object. From this example, it should be obvious that all three gunas are necessary for an act of creation. Sattwa alone would be just an unrealized idea, rajas without sattwa would be mere undirected energy, rajas without tamas would be like a lever without a fulcrum.

If we wish to describe the gunas individually, we can say that sattwa represents all that is pure, ideal and tranquil, while rajas expresses itself in action, motion and violence, and tamas is the principle of solidity, immobile resistance and inertia. As has been said above, all three gunas are present in everything, but one guna always predominates. Sattwa, for example, predominates in sunlight, rajas in the erupting volcano, and tamas in a block of granite. In the mind of man, the gunas are usually found in a relationship of extreme instability—hence the many moods through which we pass in the course of a single day. Sattwa causes our moments of inspiration, disinterested affection, quiet joy and meditative calm. Rajas brings on our outbursts of rage and fierce desire. It makes us restless and discontented, but it is also responsible for our better phases of constructive activity, energy, enthusiasm and physical courage. Tamas is the mental bog into which we sink whenever sattwa and rajas cease to prevail. In the state of tamas, we exhibit our worst qualities—sloth, stupidity, obstinacy and helpless despair. Several chapters of the Bhagavad Gita are devoted to the gunas and their manifestations. The spiritual aspirant is advised to transcend them by a discipline of discrimination. We have already described this discipline in discussing Patanjali's aphorisms on the thought-waves—for the thought-waves are, of course, projections of the guna-forces. As the Gita puts it: "A man is said to have transcended the gunas when he does not hate the light of sattwa, or the activity of rajas, or even the delusion of tamas, while these prevail; and yet does not long for them after they have ceased. He is like one who sits unconcerned, and is not disturbed by the gunas. He knows that they are the doers of all action, and never loses this power of discrimination. He rests in the inner calm of the Atman, regarding happiness and suffering as one."

We have seen that the interaction of the gunas provides the motive power for the creative process. Now we can consider its stages. In the Hindu system, the first stage of evolution from undifferentiated Prakriti is called *mahat*, "the great cause." Mahat is the cosmic ego-sense, the first drawing of differentiated consciousness. It may perhaps be compared to the Spirit moving on the face of the waters which is mentioned in the Book of Genesis. From mahat is evolved buddhi, the discriminating faculty which has already been described. From buddhi is evolved ahamkara, the individual ego-sense. From ahamkara, the lines of evolution branch off in three different directions—to produce manas, the recording faculty; the five powers of perception (sight, smell, hearing, taste and touch); the five organs of action (tongue, feet, hands and the organs of evacuation and procreation); and the five *tanmatras*, which are the subtle inner essences of sound, feelings, aspect, flavour and odour.

These subtle tanmatras, combining and recombining, are then said to produce the five gross elements—earth, water, fire, air and ether, of which the external universe is composed.

To sum all this up briefly, creation is here described as an evolution outward, from undifferentiated into differentiated consciousness, from mind into matter. Pure consciousness is, as it were, gradually covered by successive layers of ignorance and differentiation, each layer being grosser and thicker than the one below it, until the process ends on the outer physical surface of the visible and tangible world.

It is necessary to keep this idea of evolution clearly in mind if we are to understand Patanjali's technique of meditation. For meditation is evolution in reverse. Meditation is a process of devolution. Beginning at the surface of life, the meditative mind goes inward, seeking always the cause behind the appearance, and then the cause behind the cause, until the innermost Reality is reached.

Now let us consider Patanjali's four stages of "concentration upon a single object." This kind of concentration is contrasted with the other, higher kind of concentration which is described in the next aphorism—the concentration which goes deeper than all objects and unites itself with pure, undifferentiated consciousness. Concentration upon a single object is, however, a necessary preliminary stage. When it is practised intensely, it can take the mind very far, right out to the ultimate borders of undifferentiated matter.

The words used to describe the four stages of such concentration are not easy to translate, and our English equivalents are hardly satisfactory. The stage of "examination" is said to be reached when the mind becomes perfectly concentrated upon one of the gross elements. This is followed by the stage of "discrimination", when the mind pierces the outer material layer and fastens upon the tanmatra, the subtle essence within. Next comes the stage of "joyful peace", when we concentrate upon the inner powers of perception or upon the mind itself. Finally, there is the stage of "simple awareness of individuality", when we concentrate upon the ego-sense in its simplest, most elemental form—untouched by any fear or desire—knowing only that "I" am other than "this" or "that."

Such concentration is certainly difficult enough—it may take a lifetime to achieve—but it is still within Prakriti. Therefore it has its temptations and dangers. To know the inner nature of an object is to gain power over that object. As the aspirant grows in concentration he may find himself suddenly possessed of psychic powers—he may be able to heal the sick, read men's thoughts, foresee the future or control certain natural forces. The possession of such powers presents a terrible temptation to misuse them for motives of personal greed and ambition. And it is unfortunately true that many people who dabble in "the occult" are seeking them, and nothing else. Luckily for mankind, such irresponsible experimenters usually lack of the neccessary determination, so that they do not achieve very much.

What matters is purity of motive. Cocaine, in the hands of a responsible doctor, is a beneficial pain-killer; in the hands of an addict, it is a deadly destroyer of mental and physical health. Occult powers are used by a saint with discrimination and non-attachment; he never regards them as ends in themselves or takes advantage of them to further his personal desires. Christ, who healed the servant of one of his enemies in the Garden of Gethsemane, refused at the same time to protect his own life by calling on God to send "more than twelve legions of angels." But the impure and unregenerate person who acquires those powers cannot use them rightly, and sooner or later they will cause his own ruin. The fairy tales of all nations are full of symbolic warnings against trifling with the supernatural. A few wishes are granted, and then the demon, genie, or wizard turns upon his master and takes possession of him, body and soul. By the same token, the genuine spiritual aspirant cannot be harmed by any occult powers he happens to acquire, because he regards them merely as a by-product of the enlightenment he is seeking.

As for Patanjali, has attitude is strictly scientific. He describes certain techniques of meditation and their possible results. Therefore he has to speak, in due course, about the occult powers, just as a medical writer has to give information about all kinds of drugs, even those which are dangerous. But he warns us at the same time that if we are drawn to these occult powers, we shall miss the supreme goal. If therefore, we do not heed his warning, we have only ourselves to blame.

विरामप्रत्ययाभ्यासपूर्वः संस्कारशेषोऽन्यः ॥ १८ ॥

18. The other kind of concentration is that in which the consciousness contains no object — only sub-conscious impressions, which are like burnt seeds. It is attained by constantly checking the thought-waves through the practice of non-attachment.

When the spiritual aspirant has achieved the highest degree of concentration upon a single object, he is ready to attempt the supreme feat—concentration upon consciousness itself. This is the state of perfect yoga, in which one passes beyond Prakriti; beyond all object knowledge, into union with the Atman—the undifferentiated universal consciousness. The state of perfect yoga can only be entered into when the thought-waves have been stilled and the mind has been cleared of all its samskaras, both the evil and the good—when Patanjali has ceased to believe that he is Patanjali and knows that he is none other than the Atman.

Yoga philosophy teaches us that it is the samskaras that drive us from birth to birth—just as strongly rooted addiction drives a man to take a drug, over and over again, even in spite of his conscious disinclination and the efforts of his moral will. We may say, and sincerely believe, that we are weary of the world with its interrelated pleasures and pains—"the sweet and bitter fruits of the tree"— but, in fact, we are not, as long as these subconscious tendencies remain. Our desire to return and plunge once more into sense-experience is far deeper than we realize. Beside it, our physical and spiritual hangovers, our temporary fits of disgust and repentance, count for nothing. Shakespeare has described this recurring process of attraction and aversion in one of his most powerful sonnets:

Enjoy'd no sooner but despised straight;
Past reason hunted; and no sooner had,
Past reason hated, as a swallow'd bait
On purpose laid to make the taker mad....

It follows, therefore, that when the samskaras have been rooted out and destroyed—as they must be before the state of perfect yoga is achieved—there will no longer be any urge toward rebirth. He who achieves yoga is said to be "liberated." When his present life ends, he will be united with the Atman forever. However, the achievement of perfect yoga does not necessarily mean the immediate end of mortal life. Saints have reached the supreme spiritual experience and continued to live on for many years. They have continued to think, speak and act on the plane of external phenomena—but with a difference. The thoughts, words, and actions of a liberated man are said to be like "burnt seeds"—that is to say, they are no longer fertile; they cannot bring forth any more samskaras, they cannot create any new addiction or bondage.

In Sanskrit, a mental or physical act is called a *Karma*. Karma is also the word used to describe the consequence of this act, and hence to describe what we call "fate"—since our fate is nothing but the sum of the consequences of our past actions in this and previous lives. After a man has achieved liberation in yoga, his acts will cease to produce karmas. The remainder of his earthly life will be governed only by the karmas which were already in existence before his liberation. He is like an actor on the last night of a play. He knows that the play will never be performed again, no matter how well he does his part, no matter whether the audience boos or applauds. He has nothing to gain or lose by his performance. Nevertheless, he must play it through to the end until the final curtain falls and he can go home.

Speaking of the actions of one who has achieved liberation, Shankara tells us: "Such actions are performed, as it were, from memory. They are like the remembered actions of a dream."

भव-प्रत्ययो विदेह-प्रकृतिलयानाम् ॥ १९ ॥

19. When such concentration is not accompanied by non-attachment, and ignorance therefore remains, the aspirant will reach the state of the

disincarnate gods or become merged in the forces of Nature.

Concentration without non-attachment cannot bring liberation. However hard we may struggle, we can only be rewarded in accordance with our desires. If we really want liberation, and work hard enough for it, we shall get it. But if we really want power and pleasure we can get them instead—not only in this world and in this human form, but in other worlds and other forms here after. Concentration upon any of the gross elements or the sense-organs is said to bring us to the condition of disincarnate gods; concentration upon the mind or the ego is said to make us one with the forces of Nature, and rulers of parts of the universe.

If a Hindu speaks of "heaven" and "hell", he does not use the words in the accepted Christian sense. For, to a Hindu, heaven and hell are both within Prakriti. He believes in many planes of existence other than this earthly one—some infernally painful, some celestially pleasant. To these planes we may go for a while, after death, impelled by the karmas we have accumulated here on earth. But we shall not remain in any one of them eternally. When the good or the bad karma which earned them is exhausted, we shall be reborn into mortal life—the only condition, according to Hindu belief, in which we are free to make the act of yoga, to unite ourselves with the Atman.

The desire for heaven is therefore an infinitely lower ambition than the desire for liberation. All Hindu religious literature makes a clear distinction between the two. When Sri Krishna is reproving Arjuna for his preoccupation with the problems of the phenomenal world, he speaks of the man "who *merely* hopes for heaven." Note also Emerson's poem "Brahma":

The strong gods pine for my abode,
And pine in vain the sacred Seven;
But thou, meek lover of the good!
Find me, and turn thy back on heaven!

"The strong gods" are, in fact, not strong at all. They are in bondage to Prakriti, chained to this cosmos by their desire for power. They are among those who have failed to concentrate with non-attachment. In the Katha Upanishad, Yama, the god of death, admits this frankly to Nachiketa; "Well I know that earthly treasure lasts but till the morrow. For did not I myself, wishing to be King of Ḍeath, make sacrifice with fire? But the sacrifice was a fleeting thing, performed with fleeting objects, and small is my reward, seeing that only for a moment will my reign endure."

Yama knows that one day he will have to leave his kingdom and be reborn as a man. Then, and only then, he will have another opportunity to turn his back on heaven and seek that union with the Atman which is the only true immortality.

श्रद्धा-वीर्य-स्मृति-समाधि-प्रज्ञा-पूर्वक
इतरेषाम् ॥ २० ॥

20. The concentration of the true spiritual aspirant is attained through faith, energy, recollectedness, absorption and illumination.

"Faith" is often used by agnostics as a term of abuse. That is to say, it is taken to refer to the blind credulity which accepts all kinds of dogmas and creeds without question, repeating parrot-like what has been taught, and closing its ears to doubt and reason. Such "faith" should certainly be attacked. It is compounded of laziness, obstinacy, ignorance and fear. Because it is rigid and unyielding it can quite easily by shaken and altogether destroyed.

But this is not the true faith—the faith which is recommended by Patanjali. True faith is provisional, flexible, undogmatic, open to doubt and reason. True faith is not like a picture frame, a permanently limited area of acceptance. It is like a plant which keeps on throwing forth shoots and growing. All we require, at the beginning, is a seed. And the seed need be nothing more than a feeling of interest in the possibilities of the spiritual life. Perhaps we read a passage in a book which moves us. Perhaps we meet someone who seems to have reached some degree of wisdom and tranquillity through the practice of meditation and spiritual disciplines. We become interested and intrigued. Maybe this is a solution for our own problems, maybe it isn't. We can't be sure—we *ought* not, at this stage, be sure—but we decide to give it a try.

Suppose you are subject to indigestion. One day you read a book about diet or meet a doctor who tells you that he can restore your health if you follow his instructions. You do not have to accept the book or the doctor with blind faith, but you do have to have provisional, hypothetical faith. You have to *assume* that the diet will help your condition. You have to try it before you can say with authority whether it is helpful or useless. So, too, with the spiritual diet which the great teachers recommend. You have to have provisional faith in the truth of the scriptures and in the word of your teacher.

Also, you have to have energy. Without energy you cannot follow any kind of instructions, day after day, and really test their value. The Buddha pointed out that, if there is any sin, it is laziness. As we have seen in discussing the gunas, tamas is the lowest condition of nature and the human mind.

But, luckily for us, energy is like a muscle; it grows stronger through being used. This is a very simple and obvious, yet perpetually amazing truth. Every creative artist knows those days of apparently blank stupidity and lack of inspiration on which he has to force himself to work. And then, suddenly, after hours of toiling, the effort is rewarded; ideas and enthusiasm begin to flow into him. In all our undertakings, the little daily effort is all-important. The muscles of our energy must be continually exercised. Thus, gradually, we gain momentum and purpose.

As faith increases through personal experience and energy grows through practice, the mind acquires a direction. It becomes recollected, in the basic meaning of the word. Our thoughts have been scattered, as it were, all over the mental field. Now we begin to collect them again and to direct them toward a single goal—knowledge of the Atman. As we do this we find ourselves becoming increasingly absorbed in the thought of what we are seeking. And so, at length, absorption merges into illumination, and the knowledge is ours.

तीव्रसंवेगानामासन्नः ॥ २१ ॥

21. Success in yoga comes quickly to those who are intensely energetic.

मृदुमध्याधिमात्रत्वात्ततोऽपि विशेषः ॥ २२ ॥

22. Success varies according to the means adopted to obtain it — mild, medium or intense.

Theoretically, there is no reason why we should not achieve the state of perfect yoga within the space of a single second—since the Atman is eternally within us and our ignorance of this fact could be instantaneously dispelled. Practically, however, our progress is retarded by our past karmas, our present fears and desires, and the relative strength of our energy. No one can generalize about the period required—it might, in any individual case extend over months, years or lifetimes. All we can say is this—no effort, however small, is wasted, and the harder we try, the sooner we shall succeed.

ईश्वरप्रणिधानाद्वा ॥ २३ ॥

23. Concentration may also be attained through devotion to Ishwara.

क्लेशकर्मविपाकाशयैरपरामृष्टः पुरुषविशेष ईश्वरः ॥ २४ ॥

24. Ishwara is a special kind of Being, untouched by ignorance and the products of ignorance, not subject to karmas or samskaras or the results of action.

Here, for the first time, Patanjali introduces the idea of God. According to Vedanta philosophy *Ishwara* is the supreme Ruler of the universe—its Creator, Sustainer and Dissolver. Brahman, the ultimate Reality, cannot properly be said to create, sustain or dissolve, since Brahman is, by definition, without attributes. Ishwara is Brahman seen within Prakriti. He corresponds, more or less, to God the Father in the Christian tradition.

What is important is the concept of devotion. Liberation, as we have already seen, *can* be reached without devotion to God. But this is a subtle and dangerous path, threading its way through the pitfalls of ambition and pride. Devotion to a personal ideal of God brings with it a natural inclination to humility and service. It sweetens the dryness of intellectual discrimination and calls forth the highest kind of love of which man is capable. We cannot even imagine Brahman until the moment of our liberation, but we can all imagine Ishwara, according to our different natures—for Ishwara has attributes which our minds can recognize. Ishwara is all that we can know of the Reality until we pass beyond Prakriti.

If we set ourselves to serve Ishwara, if we dedicate our actions and surrender our wills to Him, we shall find that He draws us to Himself. This is the grace of God, which Sri Ramakrishna compared to an ever-blowing breeze; you have only to raise your sail in order to catch it. And in the Gita, we read:

> Whatever your action
> Food or worship;
> Whatever the gift
> That you give to another;
> Whatever you vow
> To the work of the spirit:.....
> Lay these also
> As offerings before me.

This kind of devotion requires, perhaps, a special temperament. It is not for everybody. But to be able to feel it is a very great blessing, for it is the safest and happiest way to liberation.

Ishwara, it has been said, is God as He appears within Prakriti. But it must be remembered that Ishwara is Prakriti's ruler, not its servant. That is why Patanjali describes Him as "a special kind of Being". A man is the servant of Prakriti. He is subject to ignorance of his real Self (the Atman) and to products of this ignorance—egotism, attachment to sense-objects, aversion from them (which is merely attachment in reverse) and a blind clinging to his present life: the various forms of bondage which constitute misery, and which Patanjali will discuss more fully in the second chapter of his aphorisms. Ishwara is not subject to this ignorance, or to its products.

Man is subject to the laws of birth and death, the laws of karma. Ishwara is unborn, undying. Man is subject to his samskaras—the deeply rooted tendencies which drive him or to further actions and desires. Ishwara is free from samskaras and desires. He is not involved in the results of action.

Man, it is true, may become liberated. But, even in this, he differs from Ishwara—for Ishwara was never in bondage. After liberation, man is one with Brahman. But he can never become one with Ishwara. (Indeed, the desire to become Ishwara, the Ruler of the universe, would be the most insane of all egotistical desires—it seems to be typified, in Christian literature, by the story of the fall of Lucifer.) In the state of union with Brahman, both Ishwara and His universe are transcended, since both are merely projections of Brahman.

तत्र निरतिशय सर्वज्ञत्वबीजम् ॥ २५ ॥

25. In Him, knowledge is infinite; in others it is only a germ.

स पूर्वेषामपि गुरुः कालेनानवच्छेदात् ॥ २६ ॥

26. He was the teacher even of the earliest teachers, since He is not limited by time.

These two aphorisms deal with Ishwara's attribute of omniscience. If we admit the existence of knowledge—no matter how limited—in man, we must deduce from it the existence of infinite knowledge in God. Further, granted that everybody must have a teacher, Patanjali reasons that the teacher of the first teacher can only have been God, since He alone, being timeless, was present before teachers began.

तस्य वाचकः प्रणवः ॥ २७ ॥

27. The word which express Him is Om.

तज्जपस्तदर्थभावनम् ॥ २८ ॥

28. This word must be repeated with meditation upon its meaning.

ततः प्रत्यकचेतनाधिगमोऽप्यन्तरायाभावश्च ॥ २९ ॥

29. Hence comes knowledge of the Atman and destruction of the obstacles to that knowledge.

"In the beginning was the Word," says the Gospel according to St. John, and "the Word was with God, and the Word was God." This statement echoes, almost exactly, a verse from the Rig Veda: "In the beginning was Brahman, with whom was the Word; and the Word was truly the supreme Brahman." The philosophy of the Word may be traced, in its various forms and modifications, down from the ancient Hindu scriptures through the teachings of Plato and the Stoics to Philo of Alexandria and the author of the Fourth Gospel. Perhaps an actual historical link can be proved to exist between all these succeeding schools of thought; perhaps it cannot be. The question is not very important. Truth may be rediscovered independently, in many different epochs and places. The power of the Word, for good and for evil, has been recognized by mankind since the dawn of history. Primitive tribes enshrined it in their taboos and secret cults. Twentieth-century cultures have prostituted it to the uses of politics and commercial advertisement.

Words and ideas are inseparable. You cannot have the idea of God without the word which expresses God. But why necessarily, use the word OM? The Hindus reply that, because God is the basic fact of the universe, he must be represented by the most basic, the most natural, the most comprehensive of all sounds. And they claim that this sound is OM (or AUM as it should be properly pronounced). To quote Swami Vivekananda: "The first letter, *A*, is the root sound, the key pronounced without touching any part of the tongue or palate; *M* represents the last sound in the series, being produced by the closed lip, and the *U* rolls from the very root to the end of the sounding-board of the mouth. Thus, OM represents the whole phenomena of sound-producing." If any of us feel that a mere argument from phonetics is insufficient to establish this claim, we should remember, also, that OM is almost certainly the most ancient word for God that has come down to us through the ages. It has been used by countless millions of worshippers—always in the most universal sense; implying no special attribute, referring to no one particular deity. If such use can confer sanctity, then OM is the most sacred word of all.

But what really matters is that we should appreciate the power of the Word in our spiritual life; and this appreciation can come only through practical experience. People who have never tried the practice of repeating the name of God are apt to scoff at it: it seems to them so empty, so mechanical. "Just repeating the same word over and over!" they exclaim scornfully. "What possible good can that do?"

The truth is that we are all inclined to flatter ourselves — despite our daily experience to the contrary — that we spend our time thinking logical, consecutive thoughts. In fact, most of us do no such thing. Consecutive thought about any one problem occupies a very small proportion of our waking hours. More usually, we are in a state of reverie — a mental fog of disconnected sense-impressions, irrelevant memories, non-sensical scraps of sentences from books and newspapers, little darting fears and resentments, physical sensations of discomfort, excitement or ease. If, at any given moment, we could take twenty human minds and inspect their workings, we should probably find one, or at most two, which were functioning rationally. The remaining eighteen or nineteen minds would look more like this: "Ink-bottle. That time I saw Roosevelt. In love with the night mysterious. Reds veto Pact. Jimmy's trying to get my job. Mary says I'm fat. Big toe hurts. Soup good......." etc., etc. Because we do nothing to control this reverie, it is largely conditioned by external circumstances. The weather is cloudy, so our mood is sad. The sun comes out, our mood brightens. Insects begin to buzz around us, and we turn irritable and nervous. Often, it is as simple as that.

But now, if we introduce into this reverie the repetition of the name of God, we shall find that we can control our moods, despite the interference of the outside world. We are always, anyhow, repeating words in our minds — the name of a friend or an enemy, the name of an anxiety, the name of a desired object — and each of these words is surrounded by its own mental climate. Try saying "war," or "money," ten thousand times, and you will find that your whole mood has been changed and coloured by the associations connected with that word. Similarly, the name of God will change the climate of your mind. It cannot do otherwise.

In the Hindu scriptures we often find the phrase: "To take refuge in His name." (See also the Book of Proverbs, xviii, 10: "The name of the Lord is a strong tower: the righteous runneth into it and is safe.") This phrase — which at first may sound rather too poetical — comes to have a very real and literal significance in our spiritual life. When the mind is so violently disturbed by pain or fear or the necessities of some physical emergency that it cannot possibly be used for meditation or even rational thought, there is still one thing that you can always do; you can repeat His name, over and over. You can hold fast to that, throughout all the tumult. Once you have really tested and proved the power of the holy Word, you will rely upon it increasingly. Through constant practice, the repetition becomes automatic. It no longer has to be consciously willed. It is rather like the thermostat on a water heater or a refrigerator. Whenever the mind reaches an undesirable "temperature" you will find that the repetition begins of itself and continues as long as it is necessary.

Mere repetition of God's name is, of course, insufficient — as Patanjali points out. We must also meditate upon its meaning. But the one process follows naturally upon the other. If we persevere in our repetition, it will lead us inevitably into meditation. Gradually, our confused reverie will give way to concentrated thought. We cannot long continue to repeat any word without beginning to think about the reality which it represents. Unless we are far advanced in spiritual practice, this concentration will not be maintained for more than a few moments; the mind will slip back into reverie again. But it will be a higher kind of reverie — a reverie dominated by sattwa rather than by rajas or tamas. And the Name, perpetually uttered within it, will be like a gentle plucking at our sleeve, demanding and finally recapturing our attention.

In India, when a disciple comes to his teacher for initiation, he is given what is called a *mantram*. The *mantram* consists of one or more holy names which the disciple is to repeat and meditate upon, throughout the rest of his life. It is regarded as very private and very sacred — the essence, as it were, of the teacher's instructions to that particular disciple, and the seed within which spiritual wisdom is passed down from one generation to another. You must never tell your *mantram* to any other human being. The act of repeating it is called *japam*. You can make *japam* aloud if you are alone, or silently if you are among other people. It is convenient to do this with a rosary — thus linking thought with physical action (which is one of the great advantages of all ritual) and providing a small but sufficient outlet for the nervous energy of the body, which might otherwise accumulate and disturb the mind. Most spiritual aspirants resolve to make a certain fixed amount of *japam* everyday. The rosary serves to measure this — one bead to each repetition of the *mantram* — so that you are not distracted by having to count.

Needless to add, the practice of making *japam* is not confined to the Hindu religion. The Catholics teach it also. "Hail Mary" is a *mantram*. A form of *mantram* is also recognised by the Greek Orthodox Church. We quote here form those two remarkable books, *The way of a Pilgrim* and *The Pilgrim Continues His Way*, which record the spiritual pilgrimage of a Russian monk during the middle of the last century.

"The continuous interior Prayer of Jesus is a constant uninterrupted calling upon the divine Name of Jesus with the lips, in the spirit, in the heart; while forming a mental picture of his constant presence, and imploring his grace, during every occupation, at all times, in all places, even during sleep. The appeal is couched in these terms, "Lord Jesus Christ, have mercy on me." One who accustoms himself to this appeal experiences as a result so deep a consolation and so great a need to offer the prayer always, that he can no longer live without it, and it will continue to voice itself within him of its own accord."

Many so-called enlightened people regard this frequent offering of one and the same prayer as useless and even trifling, calling it mechanical and a thoughtless occupation of simple people. But unfortunately they do not know the secret which is revealed as a result of this mechanical exercise, they do not know how this frequent service of the lips imperceptibly becomes a genuine appeal of the heart, sinks down into the inward life, becomes a delight, becomes as it were, natural to the soul, bringing it light and nourishment and leading it on to union with God.

St. John Chrysostom, in his teaching about prayer, speaks as follows:

"No one should give the answer that it is impossible for a man occupied with worldly cares, and who is unable to go to church, to pray always. Everywhere, wherever you may find yourself, you can set up an altar to God in your mind by means of prayers. And so it is fitting to pray at your trade, on a journey, standing at the counter or sitting at your handicraft....... In such an order of life all his actions, by the power of the invocation of the Name of God, would be signalized by success, and finally he would train himself to the uninterrupted prayerful invocation of the Name of Jesus Christ. He would come to know from experience that frequency of prayer, this sole means of salvation, is a possibility for the will of man, that it is possible to pray at all times, in all circumstances and in every place, and easily to rise from frequent vocal prayer to prayer of the mind and from that to prayer of the heart, which opens up the Kingdom of God within us."

व्याधि-स्त्यान-संशय-प्रमादालस्याविरति-
भ्रान्तिदर्शनालब्धभूमिकत्वानवस्थितत्वानि
चित्तविक्षेपास्तेऽन्तरायाः ॥ ३० ॥

30. Sickness, mental laziness, doubt, lack of enthusiasm, sloth, craving for sense-pleasure, false perception, despair caused by failure to concentrate and unsteadiness in concentration: these distractions are the obstacles to knowledge.

दुःख-दौर्मनस्याङ्गमेजयत्व-श्वासप्रश्वासा
विक्षेपसहभुवः ॥ ३१ ॥

31. These distractions are accompanied by grief, despondency, trembling of the body and irregular breathing.

It will be noticed that nearly all distractions listed by Patanjali come under the general heading of tamas. Sloth is the great enemy — the inspirer of cowardice, irresolution, self-pitying grief, and trivial, hair-splitting doubts. Sloth may also be a psychological cause of sickness. It is tempting to relax from our duties, take refuge in ill-health and hide under a nice warm blanket. The body resists all unaccustomed disciplines, and will perhaps try to sabotage them by alarming, hysterical displays of weakness, fainting spells, violent headaches, palpitations, and so forth. This resistance is subconscious. The symptoms it produces are genunine enough. It is no good trying to fight them by sheer force — dragging yourself out of bed and staggering around in a fever. But you can attack your sloth on the subconscious level by quiet persistence in making japam. You are never too weak or too sick for that. And sloth will relax its hold upon you, little by little, when it understands that you really mean business.

When an aspirant enters upon the spiritual life, he naturally does so with great enthusiasm. The first steps he takes are almost always accompanied by feelings of peace and delight. Everything seems so easy, so inspiring. It is therefore very important that he should realize, right from the start, that this mood will not continue, uninterrupted, throughout the rest of his course. Religion is not simply a state of euphoria. There will be relapses; phases of struggle, dryness, and doubt. But these ought not to distress him unduly. Conscious feelings, however exalted, are not the only indications of spiritual progress. We may be growing most strongly at a time when our minds seem dark and dull. So we should never listen to the promptings of sloth, which will try to persuade us that this dullness is a sign of failure. There is no failure as we continue to make an effort.

तत्प्रतिषेधार्थमेकतत्वाभ्यास: ॥ ३२ ॥

32. They can be removed by the practice of concentration upon a single truth.

That is to say, the truth of God's existence. God has many aspects, and so there are innumerable approaches to him. Patanjali will deal with some of them, later, in detail. This aphorism simply stresses the importance of single-mindedness. When the aspirant has chosen his ideal form of the Godhead and his way of approaching it, he must hold fast to that. Some people are apt to be too catholic in their attitude to religion; they try a little of this cult, a little of that, and fail to follow any one path through to the goal where all are united. Sri Ramakrishna compared them to the man who digs a number of shallow wells, but never goes deep enough to find water anywhere.

In order to achieve this concentration, we must calm and purify our minds. Patanjali now tells us how to do this. He prescribes the mental attitude we should take toward our neighbours in this world.

मैत्री-करुणामुदितोपेक्षाणां सुखदुःखपुण्यापुण्य-
विषयाणां भावनातश्चित्तप्रसादनम् ॥ ३३ ॥

33. Undisturbed calmness of mind is attained by cultivating friendliness toward the happy, compassion for the unhappy, delight in the virtuous, and indifference toward the wicked.

If we meet someone who is happy in his way of life, we are inclined to envy him and be jealous of his success. We must learn to rejoice in it, as we take pleasure in the happiness of a friend. If someone is unhappy, we should feel sorry for him, instead of despising him or criticising him for bringing misfortunes upon himself. The virtue of others is apt to irritate us, because we take it as a reflection upon our own shortcomings. We are tempted to sneer at it and suggest that it is only hypocrisy. On the contrary, we should delight in it and see it as an inspiration to ourselves to do better. As for the wicked, we must remember Christ's words: "Be not overcome of evil." If someone harms us or hates us, our first instinct is to answer him with hatred and injury. We may succeed in injuring him, but we shall be injuring ourselves much more, and our hatred will throw our own minds into confusion. So we must practise indifference toward the hurts we receive from others. We must go behind the wickedness of the wicked and try to understand what makes them treat us in that way. Very often we shall discover that we ourselves are partly to blame for their attitude. The relationship between the aggressor and his victim, the murderer and the murdered, is not always one of simple guilt and innocence; it may be very complex. There may be provocation on both sides.

Our proper approach toward our fellow human beings is summed up in one of the first of the Hindu monastic vows: "The bees seek honey. I will shun the habit of the flies and follow that of the bees. I will refrain from finding faults in others and look only for the good which is in them." That is a vow which we should all take and try to live up to.

प्रच्छर्दन-विधारणाभ्यां वा प्राणस्य॰ ॥ ३४ ॥

34. The mind may also be calmed by expulsion and retention of the breath.

The word used here by Patanjali is *prana.* Prana actually means energy — the vital energy which we draw into ourselves from the surrounding universe. Since this energy is obtained primarily by breathing, we may translate prana as "breath" in this particular context.

Later on, we shall learn more about the system of breathing exercises to which Patanjali refers. It is known as *pranayama.* But, without going into details, it is necessary to make two general observations here.

First, we must note that Patanjali sees control of the mind as a psychophysical problem. In this he agrees with modern scientific thought. Studies of breathing have shown that the method of respiration affects the whole organism. Calmness can actually be induced by deep steady inhalations and exhalations. Mental disturbance and despondency are accompanied (as Patanjali notes in aphorism 31 of this chapter) by irregular breathing; rapid, shallow and uncontrolled.

Secondly, it must never be forgotten that pranayama is merely a physical means to a spiritual end. Many uninformed people imagine that yoga is nothing but a system of breathing exercises and complicated postures — "holding your breath and standing on your head." When they speak of "yoga" they really only mean *hatha yoga*, which is the correct name for this system of exercises, as originally practised in ancient India. Hatha yoga was designed to prepare the aspirant for spiritual experience by perfecting his body; but it has been condemned by spiritual teachers because it tends, in practice, to concentrate the mind upon the body itself. In the West, it is to be found in a completely degenerated form, as a cult of physical beauty and prolonged youth. As such, it may be effective, certainly, but also dangerous. Overindulgence in breathing exercises, just for the sake of the agreeable "oxygen-jag" which they produce, may lead to hallucinations and, possibly, insanity. And, even at best, an excessive preoccupation with our physical appearance and well-being is obviously a distraction, causing us to forget, in silly vanity, our proper purpose.

विषयवती वा प्रवृत्तिरुत्पन्ना मनसः
स्थितिनिबन्धिनी ॥ ३५ ॥

35. Those forms of concentration which result in extra-ordinary perceptions encourage perseverance of the mind.

Because most of us are naturally sceptical, despite our affirmed "beliefs," we need to be reassured that the powers of mind over matter really exist. Despite countless, well-documented experiments, carried out under the strictest laboratory conditions, we still smile apologetically when we speak of telepathy, precognition and the phenomena of mediumship. If we have studied the subject at all, we cannot exactly disbelieve that such things are possible, but still — they haven't happened to *us.* Until they do, the mind harbours its little germ of doubt.

Patanjali therefore recommends that we shall try to develop some "extraordinary perceptions" for ourselves. We are told that if a man concentrates on the tip of his nose he will smell wonderful perfumes. If concentration is fixed on the tip of the tongue, a supernormal sense of taste will result; if on the palate, a supernormal sense of colour; if on the middle of the tongue, a supernormal sense of touch; if on the root of the tongue, a supernormal sense of hearing. Such powers are of no value in themselves, but they at least serve to prove what can be done with the mind, just as acrobatic tricks in a gymnasium prove how powerful and flexible a trained human body can become. Thus we begin to understand that everything is possible to those who can concentrate, and so we are encouraged to persevere, to break through the barriers of ordinary sense-perception and to press forward fearlessly in our search for inner knowledge. The physical strength gained in a gymnasium can be used later for practical purposes. The mental strength gained through these exercises in concentration can be used for the most practical purpose of all; to unite ourselves with the Atman.

विशोका वा ज्योतिष्मती ॥ ३६ ॥

36. Concentration may also be attained by fixing the mind upon the Inner Light, which is beyond sorrow.

The ancient yogis believed that there was an actual centre of spiritual consciousness, called "the lotus of the heart," situated between the abdomen and the thorax, which could be revealed in deep meditation. They claimed that it had the form of a lotus and that it shone with an inner light. It was said to be "beyond sorrow," since those who saw it were filled with an extraordinary sense of peace and joy.

From the very earliest times, the masters of yoga emphasized the importance of meditating upon this lotus. "The supreme heaven shines in the lotus of the heart," says the Kaivalya Upanishad, "Those who struggle and aspire may enter there. Retire into solitude. Seat yourself on a clean spot in an erect posture, with the head and neck in a straight line. Control all sense-organs. Bow down in devotion to your teacher. Then enter the lotus of the heart and meditate there on the presence of Brahman — the pure, the infinite, the blissful."

And in the Chandogya Upanishad we read:

> Within the city of Brahman, which is the body, there is the heart, and within the heart there is a little house. This house has the shape of a lotus, and within it dwells that which is to be sought after inquired about, and realized.
>
> What, then, is that which dwells within this little house, this lotus of the heart? What is it that must be sought after, inquired about, and realized?
>
> Even so large as the universe outside is the universe within the lotus of the heart. Within it are heaven and earth, the sun, the moon, the lightning and all the stars. Whatever is in the macrocosm is in this microcosm also.
>
> All things that exist, all beings and all desires, are in the city of Brahman; what, then, becomes of them when old age approaches and the body dissolves in death?
>
> Though old age comes to the body, the lotus of the heart does not grow old. It does not die with the death of the body. The lotus of the heart, where Brahman resides in all his glory

that, and not the body, is the true city of Brahman. Brahman, dwelling therein, is untouched by any deed, ageless, deathless, free from grief, free from hunger and from thirst. His desires are right desires, and his desires are fulfilled.

And in the Mundaka Upanishad: "Within the lotus of the heart he dwells, where the nerves meet like the spokes of a wheel. Meditate upon him as OM, and you may easily cross the ocean of darkness. In the effulgent lotus of the heart dwells Brahman, passionless and indivisible. He is pure. He is the light of all lights. The knowers of Brahman attain him."

This method of meditation is helpful, because it localizes our image of the spiritual consciousness toward which we are struggling. If the body is thought of as a busy and noisy city, then we can imagine that, in the middle of this city, there is a little shrine, and that, within this shrine, the Atman, our real nature, is present. No matter what is going on in the streets outside, we can always enter that shrine and worship. It is always open.

वीतरागविषयं वा चित्तम् ॥ ३७ ॥

37. Or by meditating on the heart of an illumined soul, that is free from passion.

Let your mind dwell on some holy personality — a Buddha, a Christ, a Ramakrishna. Then concentrate upon his heart. Try to imagine how it must *feel* to be a great saint; pure and untroubled by sense-objects, a knower of Brahman. Try to feel that the saint's heart has become your heart; within your own body. Here, again, the localization of the image will be found very helpful. Both Hindus and Christians practise this form of meditation — concentrating not only upon the heart but also, sometimes, upon the hands and the feet and the whole form.

स्वप्ननिद्राज्ञानालम्बनं वा ॥ ३८ ॥

38. Or by fixing the mind upon a dream experience, or the experience of deep sleep.

By "a dream experience" Patanjali means a dream about a holy personality or a divine symbol. Such dreams can properly be called experiences, because they bring a sense of joy and revelation which remains with us after we have awaked. In the literature of Indian spirituality we find many instances of devotees who dreamed that they received a mantram from some great teacher. Such a dream-mantram is regarded as being just as sacred as one which is given in the waking state, and the devotee who receives it will continue to use it and meditate upon it throughout the rest of his life.

Another method of calming the mind is to concentrate upon that sense of peaceful happiness with which we awake from deep, dreamless sleep. According to Vedanta philosophy, the Atman in man is covered by three layers or "sheaths." The outermost of these is the physical sheath, which is the layer of gross matter. Below this is the subtle sheath which is composed of the inner essence of things, and is the stuff of the spirit world. Below this is the causal sheath, so called because it is the web of our karma, the complex of cause and effect which makes our personalities and our lives what they are at any given moment. The causal sheath is the ego-sense which makes us see ourselves and the phenomena of the universe as separate entities. In the waking state, Vedanta tells us, all of these three sheaths come between us and the Atman, but in dreamless sleep the two outer coverings are removed and only the casual sheath, the ego-sense, remains. It follows, therefore, that we are nearer to the Atman in dreamless sleep than in any other phase of our ordinary unspiritual lives; nearer – yet still so far, for what separates us is the toughest covering of the three, the basic layer of our ignorance, the lie of otherness. And this sheath can never be broken through by mere sleeping. We cannot hope to wake up one morning and find ourselves united with Reality. Nevertheless, some faint hint, some slight radiation of the joyful peace of the Atman *does* come through to us in this state, and remains with us when we return to waking consciousness. We should try to hold it and dwell within it. It is a foretaste of the bliss of perfect knowledge.

यथाभिमतध्यानाद्वा ॥ ३९ ॥

39. Or by fixing the mind upon any divine form or symbol that appeals to one as good.

One of the most attractive characteristics of Patanjali's philosophy is its breadth of vision, its universality. There is no attempt here to impose any particular cult upon the light of his presence — no matter how dimly it shines through the layers of our ignorance — that we fashion our own pictures and symbols of goodness and project them upon the outside world. Every such picture, symbol, or idea is holy, if it is conceived in sincerity. It may be crude and childish, it may not appeal to others; that is unimportant. All-important is our attitude toward it. Whatever we truly and purely worship, we make sacred.

Therefore, we should always feel reverence for the religions of others, and beware of bigotry. At the same time, however — as has been remarked above in reference to aphorism 32 — we must limit ourselves to one way of seeking and keep to that; otherwise we shall waste all our energies in mere spiritual "window-shopping." We can find nothing in a shrine or a place of pilgrimage if we bring nothing into it, and we must never forget, in the external practice of a cult, that, though the Reality is everywhere, we can only make contact with it in our own hearts.

As the great Hindu saint Kabir says in one of his most famous poems.

> I laugh when I hear that the fish
> in the water is thirsty.
> You wander restlessly from forest
> to forest while the Reality
> is within your own dwelling.
> The truth is here! Go where you will—
> to Benares or to Mathura;
> until you have found God
> in your own soul, the whole world
> will seem meaningless to you.

परमाणु-परममहत्त्वान्तोऽस्य वशीकारः ॥ ४० ॥

40. The mind of a yogi can concentrate upon any object of any size, from the atomic to the infinitely great.

"A yogi," here, does not merely mean "one who practises yoga," but one who has already achieved the power of undivided ("one-pointed") concentration. This power can, of course, only be achieved through complete self-mastery. When a spiritual aspirant begins to practise concentration, he meets all sorts of distractions. You never realize how much junk you have in the house until you start to clear out the attic and the cellar. You never realize how much rubbish has accumulated in the subconscious region of your mind, until you make the attempt to concentrate. Many beginners therefore become discouraged. "Before I started to practise concentration," they say, "my mind seemed fairly clean and calm. Now it's disturbed and full of dirty thoughts.

It disgusts me. I'd no idea I was that bad! And surely I'm getting worse, not better!" They are wrong, of course. The very fact that they have undertaken a mental housecleaning, and stirred up all this mess, means that they have taken a step in the right direction. As for the calmness which they imagine they have hitherto experienced, it was nothing but apathy — the stillness of a pool which is choked with mud. To the casual observer, sloth and serenity — tamas and sattwa — may sometimes look alike. But to pass from the one to the other, we have to go through the violent disturbance of active effort — the phase of rajas. The casual observer, watching our struggles and our distress, may say: "He used to be much easier to get along with. I liked him better the way he was. Religion doesn't seem to agree with him." We must not mind that. We must continue our struggle, with all its temporary humiliations, until we reach that self-mastery, that one-pointedness of concentration, of which Patanjali speaks.

क्षीणवृत्तेरभिजातस्येव मणेर्ग्रहीतृ-ग्रहण-ग्राह्येषु
तत्स्थतदञ्जनता समापत्तिः ॥ ४१ ॥

41. Just as the pure crystal takes color from the object which is nearest to it, so the mind, when it is cleared of thought-waves, achieves sameness or identity with the object of its concentration. This may be either a gross object, or the organ of perception, or the sense of ego. This achievement of samness or identity with the object of cencentration is known as samadhi.

The various objects of concentration here referred to have already been discussed in the commentary upon aphorism 17 of this chapter. The state of yoga (which

Patanjali now calls by its technical name, *samadhi*) may be achieved on each succeeding level of phenomena; we may begin with the outwardness of objects and penetrate toward the utmost inwardness of individuality. There are, therefore, various kinds of samadhi, as we shall see in a moment. But no kind of samadhi is possible until the mind has acquired this tremendous power of concentration which can achieve "sameness or identity" with its object. As we have seen, in considering aphorism 5, the thought-waves in the mind can only be stilled by first swallowing up all the many little waves in one great wave, one single object of concentration.

In the Upanishads, we find this process described in a slightly different, and perhaps simpler, manner. We are told to concentrate upon an object, any object, and to regard it as a symbol of the indwelling Reality, the Atman. If we hold fast to this concept and do not let go for a moment, we shall pass beyond the object's outer coverings of appearance to the inner nature of its being.

तत्र शब्दार्थज्ञानविकल्पैः सङ्कीर्णा सवितर्का
समापत्तिः ॥ ४२ ॥

42. When the mind achieves identity with a gross object of concentration, mixed with awareness of name, quality and knowledge, this is called savitarka samadhi.

स्मृतिपरिशुद्धौ स्वरूपशून्येवार्थमात्रनिर्भासा
निर्वितर्का ॥ ४३ ॥

43. When the mind achieves identity with a gross object of concentration, unmixed with awareness of name, quality and knowledge, so that the object alone remains, this is called nirvitarka samadhi.

All our ordinary awareness is compounded, as Patanjali says, of "name," "quality" and "knowledge." For example, when we look at a desk, we are aware (1) of the name of the object ("desk"), (2) of the quality of object (its size, shape, color,. woodenness, etc.), and (3) of our own knowledge of the object (the fact that it is we ourselves who are perceiving it). Through intense concentration we may become identified with the desk and yet still retain a mixture of "name," "quality" and "knowledge" in the mind. This is the lowest kind of samadhi, known as *savitarka*, which means "with deliberation." The term savitarka is only applied when the object of concentration belongs to the order of the gross elements, the most external order of phenomena.

In the samadhi called *nirvitarka* ("without deliberation") we reach a higher stage. Our achievement of identity with the object of concentration is now unmixed with awareness of name, quality and knowledge. Or, to put it in another way, we are at last able to still the thought-waves which are our reactions to the object, and to know nothing but the object itself, as it truly is: "the thing-in-itself", to use Kant's famous term. Kant maintained, quite rightly, that the "thing-in-itself" cannot possibly be known by the senses or the reasoning mind, since the senses and the reason can only present us with their own subjective reactions. "It remains completely unknown to us," he wrote, "what objects may be by themselves and apart from the receptivity of our senses. We know nothing but our manner of perceiving them; that manner being peculiar to us, and not necessarily shared by every being...." Kant, who did not admit the validity of any experience other than that of the senses or the reasons, was therefore forced to conclude that the"thing-in-itself" is unknowable. Here, Patanjali disagrees with him. Patanjali tells us that there is a higher kind of knowledge, a transcendental knowledge, beyond sense-perception, by which the "thing-in-itself" *can* be known. And this is, of course, the fundamental claim made by the practising mystics of every religion.

एतयैव सविचारा निर्विचारा च सूक्ष्मविषया
व्याख्याता ॥ ४४ ॥

44. When the object of concentration is a subtle object, two kinds of samadhi, called savichara and nirvichara, may be distinguished in the same manner.

That is to say, when we are dealing with objects of concentration belonging to the orders of subtle or essential phenomena (see aphorism 17 of this chapter), we must still distinguish between the higher and lower kinds of samadhi. *Savichara* ("reflective") samadhi is samadhi upon a subtle object which is mixed with awareness of name, quality and knowledge. *Nirvichara* ("super-reflective") samadhi is samadhi upon a subtle object which is unmixed with such awareness.

सूक्ष्मविषयत्वञ्चालिङ्ग-पर्यवसानम् ॥ ४५ ॥

45. Behind all subtle objects is Prakriti, the primal cause.

As we have already seen, in studying Patanjali's picture of the universe, Prakriti is the elemental, undifferentiated stuff of matter; the energy by which all phenomena are projected. As the meditative mind turns inward, it probes through the gross outer coverings of things to their subtle essences; and beyond these subtle essences, it comes to Prakriti itself.

But Prakriti is not the ultimate Reality. Behind Prakriti

is Brahman. The four kinds of samadhi already described are all within the realm of phenomena, and they are only preparations for that state of direct union with Brahman which is the highest samadhi of all. In this connection, Sri Ramakrishna used to tell a parable:

> A disciple once came to a teacher to learn to meditate on God. The teacher gave him instructions, but the disciple soon returned and said that he could not carry them out; every time he tried to meditate, he found himself thinking about his pet buffalo. "Well then," said the teacher, 'you meditate on that buffalo you're so fond of." The disciple shut himself up in a room and began to concentrate on the buffalo. After some days, the teacher knocked at his door and the disciple answered: "Sir, I am sorry I can't come out to greet you. This door is too small. My horns will be in the way." Then the teacher smiled and said: "Splendid! You have become identified with the object of your concentration. Now fix that concentration upon God and you will easily succeed."

ता एव सबीजः समाधिः ॥ ४६ ॥

46. These kinds of samadhi are said to be "with seed."

That is, seeds of desire and attachment may still remain within the mind, even though perfect concentration has been achieved. And these seeds of desire are dangerous, as we saw in considering the fate of those, who concentrate without non-attachment (aphorism 19 of this chapter). However, liberation is now very near. The aspirant has already risen to such heights that it is unlikely that he will fall back into bondage.

निर्विचार-वैशारद्येऽध्यात्मप्रसादः ॥ ४७ ॥

47. In reaching nirvichara samadhi the mind becomes pure.

ऋतम्भरा तत्र प्रज्ञा ॥ ४८ ॥

48. In that samadhi, knowledge is said to be "filled with truth."

श्रुतानुमानप्रज्ञाभ्यामन्यविषया
विशेषार्थत्वात् ॥ ४९ ॥

49. The knowledge which is gained from inference and the study of scriptures is knowledge of one kind. But the knowledge which is gained from samadhi is of a much higher order. It goes beyond inference and scriptures.

Here, Patanjali describes the two kinds of knowledge: knowledge obtained through the meditation of the senses and the reason, and knowledge obtained by direct, superconscious experience. Ordinary knowledge comes to us by way of sense-perception, and the interpretation of these perceptions by our reason. Ordinary knowledge is therefore necessarily limited to "ordinary objects"; that is to say, those kinds of phenomena which are within the grasp of our sense-perceptions. When ordinary knowledge attempts to deal with what is *extra-ordinary,* its impotence is immediately revealed.

For example, we have the various scriptures and writings which tell us about the existence of God. We may read these books and accept their teachings — up to a certain point. But we cannot claim to know God because we have read them. All that we can say we know is that these scriptures were written by men who claimed to know God. Why should we believe them? True, our reason may suggest to us that the authors of the scriptures were probably honest and reliable, not self-deluded or insane, and that therefore we should be inclined to believe what they tell us. But such belief can only be partial and provisional. It is very unsatisfactory. It is certainly not knowledge.

So now we nave two alternatives. Either we must decide that there is only one kind of knowledge, limited to the objects of sense-contact, and thereby resign ourselves to a permanent agnosticism concerning the teachings of the scriptures. Or we must admit the possibility of another, a higher kind of knowledge which is supersensory and therefore capable of confirming the truth of these teachings through direct experience. Such is the knowledge which is obtained through samadhi. And each one of us has to find it for himself.

"Realization," said Swami Vivekananda, "is real religion, all the rest is only preparation — hearing lectures, or reading books, or reasoning, is merely preparing the ground; it is not religion. Intellectual assent and intellectual dissent are not religion." Religion is, infact, a severely practical and empirical kind of research. You take nothing on trust. You accept nothing but your own experience. You go forward alone, step by step, like an explorer in a virgin jungle, to see what you will find. All that Patanjali, or anybody else, can do for you is to urge you to attempt the exploration and to offer certain general hints and warnings which may be of help to you on your way.

Patanjali tells us that, in the state of nirvichara samadhi, the mind becomes "pure" and "filled with truth." The mind is said to be pure because, in this state, all the minor thought-waves have been swallowed up by one great wave of concentration upon a single object. It is true that "seeds" of attachment still exist within this wave, but only in a state of suspended animation. For the moment, at least, they can do no harm, and it is very improbable that they will ever become fertile again, because, having progressed thus far, it is comparatively easy to take the final step which will cause their annihilation.

The mind, in nirvichara samadhi, is said to be filled with truth because it now experiences direct supersensory knowledge. Those who have meditated on some Chosen Ideal or spiritual personality experience direct contact with that personality, no longer as something subjectively imagined, but as something objectively known. If you have been meditating on Krishna, or on Christ, or on Ramakrishna, and trying to picture any one of them to yourself in your imagination, you will find that your picture dissolves into the reality of a living presence. And, in knowing that presence, you will see that your picture of it was imperfect and unlike the living original. Those who have had this experience liken it to the action of a magnet. In the preliminary stages of meditation, the effort seems to come entirely from yourself; you keep forcing your mind to remain pointed at its object. But now you become aware of an outside force, a magnetic power of attractions which draws your mind in the desired direction, so that the effort is no longer your own. This is what is known as grace.

How can we be sure that the revelations obtained through samadhi are genuine revelations, and not some form of self-delusion or auto-hypnosis? Common sense suggests several tests. For instance, it is obvious that the knowledge so obtained must not contradict the knowledge which has already been obtained by others; there are many knowers but there is only one truth. Again, it is clear that this knowledge must be of something which is unknowable by other means — unknowable, that is to say, by our ordinary sense-experience. And, finally, this revelation must bring with it a complete renewal of the mind and transformation of character. "The right relation between prayer and conduct," wrote Archibishop Temple, "is not that conduct is supremely important and prayer may help it, but that prayer is supremely important and conduct tests it." And if this is true in the preliminary phases of spiritual life, it should be even more strikingly demonstrated in the final, unitive state of samadhi. In achieving that, a man becomes a saint. For, as Patanjali says:

तज्ज: संस्कारोऽन्यसंस्कारप्रतिबन्धी ॥ ५० ॥

50. The impression which is made upon the mind by that samadhi wipes out all other past impressions.

And now he goes on to tell us how to take the ultimate step into complete union with Brahman:

तस्यापि निरोधे सर्वनिरोधान्निर्बीज: समाधि: ॥ ५१ ॥

51. When the impression made by that samadhi is also wiped out, so that there are no more thought-waves at all in the mind, then one enters the samadhi which is called "seedless."

It has already been explained that samadhi is achieved by raising one object, one great wave of concentration, in the mind, by which all other thought-waves, all samskaras or past impressions, are swallowed up. But not even this one wave has to be stilled. When it has subsided, we enter that highest samadhi of all, which is called *nirvikalpa* in the Vedanta system of philosophy. Nirvikalpa samadhi is said to be seedless because it is nothing but pure, undifferentiated consciousness; it contains no phenomenal impressions whatever, no seeds of desire and attachment. Brahman is not "an object of concentration"; in Brahman is neither knower nor known. Brahman, as we have seen, is pure, undifferentiated consciousness; and so, in nirvikalpa samadhi, you are literally one with Brahman, you enter into the real nature of the apparent universe and all its forms and creatures.

It is hard to follow Patanjali to such heights, even theoretically; and perhaps it will be well, before concluding this chapter, if we go back to the beginning and try to recapitulate what he has taught us in a somewhat simpler and less technical manner.

We have to start by training the mind to concentrate, but Patanjali has warned us that this practice of concentration must be accompanied by non-attachment; otherwise we shall find ourselves in trouble. If we try to concentrate while remaining attached to the things of this world, we shall either fail altogether or our newly acquired powers of concentration will bring us into great danger, because we shall inevitably use them for selfish, unspiritual ends. Our own epoch is witnessing a terrible demonstration of the consequences of this second alternative. Twentieth-century man has concentrated upon science and technics without unlearning his attachment to nationalistic power; and so he has the secret of atomic energy — a secret which, in proper hands, would be harmless and beneficial to all, but which, in his present unregenerate state, may destroy him. The danger, as many of our more serious thinkers have pointed out, is not in the fission of the atom, it is in the human mind.

What is the simplest way to acquire non-attachment to the desires, objects and ambitions of this world? We must begin by cultivating attachment to the highest object we can conceive of, to God himself. We can do this, first of all, on the lowest level, the level of gross phenomena. Take some great spiritual teacher, a Christ, a Ramakrishna, or any major saint of any country or religion. These men actually lived on this earth in human form. You can read about their lives. You can approach them as human beings. It is easy to grow to love them, to want to be like them, to try to serve them and spread their message by modelling your life upon theirs. Through this service and this love non-attachment to other, lessor loves and objectives comes naturally. It is not that we become indifferent to other people or to our own work and duties. But our love for others is included in our Ideal; it ceases to be exclusive and possessive. And our work, because it is now done as service to that Ideal, takes on a new meaning; we shall feel more enthusiasm for it than ever before.

Through devotion to our ideal teacher and meditation upon his life, we shall gradually come to an understanding of the spirit within the man; and so we pass from the level of gross phenomena to the subtle or spiritual level. We shall no longer admire a Christ or a Ramakrishna as human beings within time, but we shall worship them as eternal, spiritual beings. We shall know them in their divine aspect. That is the second stage.

There is, however, a third stage, a third level of consciousness. For behind Christ, behind Ramakrishna, behind any conception of a personal God, there is Brahman, the Ground, the central Reality of which these figures are only partial, individual projections. When we become united with Brahman, we are united with That which was manifested in Christ and hidden within our unregenerate selves, but which is eternally present in all of us. And this union is the state of nirvikalpa samadhi.

The lower stages of samadhi all contain a vestige of the sense of duality; it is still "I" who am meditating upon "my" Ideal; there is a separation between us. And it is natural that even the great saint finds it painful to surrender this intense, personal love for his Ideal in order to achieve final, impersonal union. In describing how he first reached nirvikalpa samadhi, Sri Ramakrishna said: "Every time I gathered my mind together, I came face to face with the blissful form of Divine Mother. However much I tried to free my mind from consciousness of Mother, I didn't have the will to go beyond. But at last, collecting all the strength of my will, I cut Mother's form to pieces with the sword of discrimination, and at once my mind became "seedless," and I reached nirvikalpa. It was beyond all expression."

Nirvikalpa samadhi has been described by Shankara as follows:

> There is a continuous consciousness of the unity of Atman and Brahman. There is no longer any identification of the Atman with its coverings. All sense of duality is obliterated. There is pure, unified consciousness. The man who is well established in this consciousness is said to be illumined.
>
> A man is said to be free even in this life when he is established in illumination. His bliss is unending. He almost forgets this world of appearances.
>
> Even though his mind is dissolved in Brahman; he is fully awake, free from the ignorance of waking life. He is fully conscious, but free from any craving. Such a man is said to be free even in this life.
>
> For him, the sorrows of this world are over. Though he possesses a finite body, he remains united with the Infinite. His heart knows no anxiety. Such a man is said to be free even in this life.

Once nirvikalpa samadhi has been achieved, it is possible for the saint to pass into and out of it repeatedly. This was the case with Sri Ramakrishna. While in nirvikalpa, he experienced union with the impersonal Brahman. But, on returning to normal consciousness, he would speak of God in the aspect of the Divine Mother, his Chosen Ideal. Mother did not lose her reality for him because he had known Brahman. It is important to remember this for, in our language, the word "real" is used vaguely and loosely, and is apt to lead to confusion. When we say that Brahman alone is real, we do not mean that everything else is an illusion, but rather that Brahman alone is fundamental and omnipresent. The aspects of God, the divine incarnations, have their own relative order of reality; so do the subtle and the gross objects. The materialists — those who describe themselves as being "down to earth" — are the ones who are living in an unreal world, because they limit themselves to the level of gross sense-perception. But the perception of the illuminated saint ranges over the whole scale, from gross to subtle and from subtle to absolute; and it is only he who knows what the nature of this universe actually is.

II. YOGA AND ITS PRACTICE

तपः-स्वाध्यायेश्वरप्रणिधानानि क्रियायोगः ॥ १ ॥

1. Austerity, study, and the dedication of the fruits of one's work to God: these are the preliminary steps toward yoga.

Having devoted the first chapter of his aphorisms to the aims of yoga, Patanjali now begins a chapter on its practice. These preliminary steps toward yoga are known collectively as *kriya yoga*, which means literally "work toward yoga." The three words employed in this translation — *austerity*, *study* and *dedication* — are none of them quite self-explanatory; their Sanskrit equivalents have a somewhat different frame of reference. And so it will be necessary to elaborate on each of them in turn.

The English word "austerity" has a forbidding sound. But so have its two possible alternatives, "mortification" and "discipline." Discipline, to most of us, suggests a drill sergeant; mortification, a horrible gangrene; austerity, a cabinet minister telling the public that it must eat less butter. The puritanism which has so deeply coloured our language interferes here, as so often with our understanding of Hindu thought.

The Sanskrit word used by Patanjali in this aphorism is *tapas*, which means, in its primary sense, that which generates heat or energy. Tapas is the practice of conserving energy and directing it toward the goal of yoga, toward union with the Atman. Obviously, in order to do this, we must exercise self-discipline; we must control our physical appetites and passions. But which is psychologically misleading about the three above-mentioned English words is that they all stress the grim, negative aspect of this self-discipline instead of its joyful, positive aspect: the supreme achievement which the discipline makes possible.

To stress the negative aspect of self-discipline is to contribute to the vast amount of indirect propaganda which is made, in our society, against the spiritual life. Most people, when they speak of a monk's discipline and austerities, do so with awe and a certain horror; they find such a way of life unnatural. And yet these same people think it neither unnatural nor awe-inspiring if a young man subjects himself to equally drastic austerities in order to train for a boxing match or a race. This is because everybody can understand why one should want to win a boxing match. Why one should want to find God is much less apparent.

Austerity for austerity's sake easily degenerates into a perverse cult of self-torture, and this is another danger — that the end should be forgotten in an exaggerated cultivation of the means. In the Orient and the Occident alike, we find many exponents of such practices, with their hair shirts, knotted scourges, and beds of nails. In the Bhagavad-Gita, Sri Krishna explicitly condemns them: "You may know those men to be of demonic nature who mortify the body excessively, in ways not prescribed by the scriptures. They do this because their lust and attachment to sense-objects has filled them with egotism and vanity. In their foolishness, they weaken all their sense-organs, and outrage me, the dweller within the body."

Like the Buddha, Sri Krishna counsels moderation: "Yoga is not for the man who over-eats, or for him who fasts excessively. It is not for him who sleeps too much, or for the keeper of exaggerated vigils. Let a man be moderate in his eating and his recreation, moderately active, moderate in sleep and in wakefulness."

And, in another part of the Gita, the three kinds of true austerity are defined: "Reverence for the holy spirits, the seers, teachers and the sages; straight-forwardness, harmlessness, physical cleanliness, and sexual purity — these are the virtues whose practice is called austerity of the body. To speak without ever causing pain to another, to be truthful, to say always what is kind and beneficial, and to study the scriptures regularly — this practice is called austerity of speech. The practice of serenity, sympathy, meditation upon the Atman, withdrawal of the mind from sense-objects, and integrity of motive, is called austerity of the mind."

True austerity, in the Hindu understanding of the word, is not a process of fanatical self-punishment but of quiet and sane self-control. The body is not to be brutally beaten and broken. It is to be handled firmly but considerately, as a man handles a horse. This is the image employed by the author of the Katha Upanishad: "The senses, say the wise, are the horses; the roads they travel are the mazes of desire..... When a man lacks discrimination and his mind is uncontrolled, his senses are unmanageable, like the restive horses of a charioteer. But when a man has discrimination and his mind is controlled, his senses, like the well-trained horses of a charioteer, lightly obey the rein.... The man who has sound understanding for a charioteer and a controlled mind for reins — he it is that reaches the end of the journey."

The practice of austerity — in the sense of the Sanskrit word tapas — may also include the regular performance of ritualistic worship. But, in this connection, it is important to distinguish between the Christian and the Hindu conceptions of ritual.

Leaving out of consideration the Quakers, who exclude ritual altogether, and certain other Protestant sects who greatly minimize its importance, one may say that the Christians regard their various acts of ritual as sacraments — that is, as intrinsically beneficial and absolutely necessary acts. Being sacraments, they can only be performed by duly ordained priests or ministers. Participation in them is considered, by Catholics at least, to be vital to one's spiritual health and salvation.

To the Hindus, on the other hand, the acts of ritual are simply tokens of devotion and aids to meditation, which can be performed, if necessary, by any house-holder in his own home. They are very valuable aids, certainly — especially to a beginner — but they are by no means indispensable. If you wish, you may approach God by other paths. Much depends on the temperament of the individual devotee. No Hindu teacher would expect *all* his disciples to practise this approach.

The Hindu ritual which corresponds most nearly to the Mass or Lord's Supper is extremely elaborate, and its performance requires almost unbroken attention. For this reason, it is an excellent training for the wandering mind of the beginner. Each successive act recalls the mind to the thought behind the act. You are too busy to think of anything else. Thought and action, action and thought, form a continuous chain; and it is amazing to find what a comparatively high degree of concentration you can achieve, even from the very first. Also, ritual gives you a sense of serving God in a humble, but very direct and intimate, manner.

"It is of vital importance," said Swami Brahmananda, "that a man begins his spiritual journey from where he is. If an average man is instructed to meditate on his union with the absolute Brahman, he will not understand. He will neither grasp the truth of it nor be able to follow the instructions...... However, if that same man is asked to worship God with flowers, incense, and other accessories of the ritualistic worship, his mind will gradually become concentrated on God, and he will find joy in his worship."

"Study," in the context of this aphorism, means study of the scriptures and of other books which deal with the spiritual life. It also refers to the practice of japam, the repetition of the name of God (see chapter I, aphorism 28).

The dedication of the fruits of one's work to God is a spiritual exercise of vital importance; especially to those who are compelled by their duties to lead very active lives. It is known as *karma yoga*; the way to union with God through the performance of God-dedicated action. In following karma yoga, the devotee's whole life becomes one unending ritual; since every action is performed as an offering of devotion to God, not in the hope of one's personal gain or advantage. Needless to say, the actions done in this spirit must be "right" actions — we must never offer to God, an action which seems to us, at that particular moment and stage of our development, to be wrong. And we must work, always, to the very best of our ability; we dare not offer our second best.

To dedicate the fruits of one's work to God is to work with non-attachment. Having done the best that we know, we must not despair if our work has disappointing results, or is harshly criticized, or disregarded altogether. By the same token, we must not give way to pride and self-regarding vanity if the results of our work are successful and win popular praise. Only we can know if we have done our best, and that knowledge is our legitimate reward

All men and women of genuine greatness and personal integrity do their duty in this spirit — even though they may be professed atheists — just because it is their duty. But, if they lack devotion to God — if their ideal objective is within time and the material world — it will be almost impossible for them not to despair when they see their cause apparently defeated and their lifework brought to nothing. It is only the devotee of karma yoga who need never despair, because it is only he who is capable of absolute non-attachment towards the fruits of action. It has been said before, and it will bear constant repeating, that non-attachment is not indifference; it has nothing to do with fatalism. The fatalist is necessarily slovenly in his work. What does it matter whether he tries hard or not — what must come will come, anyway. Those critics — and they are many — who dismiss Hindu philosophy as "fatalistic" show thereby their complete failure to understand the spirit of karma yoga. The fatalist's attitude towards the results of his work is not non-attachment; it is indifference born of weakness, laziness and cowardice. If, by some stroke of luck, he wins a little unearned success, his fatalism will disappear in a flash. He will not thank "fate" for his good fortune. On the contrary, we shall hear him proclaiming to all the world how well he has worked for his objective and how deservedly he has gained it.

समाधि-भावनार्थः क्लेश-तनूकरणार्थश्च ॥ २ ॥

2. Thus we may cultivate the power of concentration and remove the obstacles to enlightenment which cause all our sufferings.

अविद्यास्मिता-राग-द्वेषाभिनिवेशाः क्लेशाः ॥३ ॥

3. These obstacles—the causes of man's sufferings—are ignorance, egoism, attachment, aversion, and the desire to cling to life.

अविद्याक्षेत्रमुत्तरेषां प्रसुप्त-तनु-
विच्छिन्नोदाराणाम् ॥ ४ ॥

4. Ignorance creates all the other obstacles. They may exist either in a potential or a vestigial form, or they may have been temporarily overcome or fully developed.

Austerity, study, and the dedication of the fruits of one's work to God are, as we saw in the preceding aphorism, the three preliminary steps toward that power of concentration which makes possible the state of perfect yoga. That is their positive value. But they have a negative value also which is equally important. They are the means of removing the obstacles to concentration and enlightenment which exist within our minds.

The word "obstacle" is worth considering, because it suggests a difference in emphasis which distinguishes Hindu from Christian thought on this subject. When a Christian speak of a "sin" he means, generally, positive act of disobedience and ingratitude toward God — and by "God" he means God the Father, the Reality as it appears within time and space in the aspect of Parent and Creator of the universe, whom Hindus call Ishwara. (See chapter I, aphorism 23.) When Patanjali speaks of an "obstacle" he refers, rather, to the negative effect which follows such an act — the whirling dust cloud of ignorance which then arises and obscures the light of the Atman within us. That is to say, Christian thought emphasizes the offence against Ishwara, who is other than ourselves; while Hindu thought emphasizes the offence against our own true nature, which is the Atman.

The difference is not fundamental, but it is important. The value of the Christian approach is that it heightens our sense of the significance and enormity of sin by relating it to a Being whom we have every reason to love and obey, our Creator and Father. The value of the Hindu approach is that it presents the consequences of sin in their ultimate aspect, which is simply alienation from the Reality within us.

Both approaches have, of course, their characteristic dangers if not properly understood. The danger of the Hindu approach lies in our psychological inability to imagine the Atman in the way that we all imagine Ishwara, more or less. It is easy to feel contrition for an offence against Ishwara and to resolve, for the time being at least, not to repeat it. But the offence of erecting obstacles against the enlightening Atman is not so immediately evident, because we are perpetually slipping back into the confusion of identifying the Atman with our ego. For example, we say kindly, almost approvingly, of an habitual drunkard or dope addict, "He was nobody's enemy but his own," and do not realize what tragic nonsense this statement is. It is only occasionally that a sense of our alienation from the Ground and Refuge of our being comes over us in a huge wave of wretchedness. ("How far art Thou from me," cried a great saint, "who am so near to Thee!") The Hindu must therefore beware of taking his sins too lightly, of relapsing into an easy optimism based on the doctrine of reincarnation. He must beware of thinking, "After all, I'm really the Atman, and I have millions of lives ahead of me — as many as I want. I'll get around to knowing my real nature sooner or later, What's the hurry?" This is the attitude which is condemned by Augustine in his *Confessions*: "I, miserable young man, had entreated chastity of Thee, and said, 'Grant me chastity and continence — but not yet.'"

The danger of the Christian approach is exactly opposite, Christianity, being predominantly dualistic, stresses the importance of Ishwara and minimizes the reality of the underlying, indwelling Atman of which Ishwara is the projection. The value of such dualistic thinking is that it teaches us devotion to God; its danger is that it may incline us to exaggerated self-loathing and impotent despair. God the Father is so awe-inspiring and just, Christ is so pure and good — and we are foul and hopeless sinners. And so we relapse into the lowest condition of egoism, identifying ourselves with our own weaknesses and feeling that we cannot escape them. We wallow in a passive mud bath of guilt, forgetting our divine nature and the obligation it imposes upon us to struggle toward self-knowledge. Here, Patanjali can help the sin-obsessed Christian. For his word, "obstacle" is a good, accurate, unsentimental word which immediately suggests a course of positive action. You don't lie down under obstacles and pity yourself. You go to work to remove them.

The use of the word "sin" is misleading also for another reason. Sin is only one-half of a concept; it has to be completed by punishment. This is unfortunate because, in the relative world, many sins appear to go unpunished. Hence arises the deadly fallacy that God may perhaps be tricked; that one may be able, now and then, to "get away with murder." The literature of Christianity is loud with complaints that the unrighteous are flourishing like the green bay tree and that nothing is being done about it. And so people resort to superstitious fancies that earthquakes, floods and famines are God's deliberate punishments for collective acts of sin.

Divine justice comes to be represented as an incalculable, spasmodic, hit-or-miss affair — which is, indeed, utterly unjust.

The use of the word "obstacle" does away with such misconceptions in a moment. It clears up any possible confusion of spiritual punishment with the punishments inflicted by Nature or by man. If you commit a murder you will probably, but not certainly, be arrested. If you build your city on an earthquake fault, or neglect your dams or your agriculture, you will probably, but not certainly, be visited with earthquakes, floods or famines. That has nothing whatever to do with the spiritual consequences of sin. Sin has only one spiritual consequence, and this is invariable and unescapable. It creates an obstacle to enlightenment — great or small, according to its magnitude — and this obstacle is its own automatic, self-contained punishment, alienation from the Atman, identification with the ego, and resultant suffering. This punishment may not be apparent to us at the moment when we incur it, but we cannot by any means escape its effects.

If you judge your thoughts and actions from Patanjali's viewpoint — asking yourself, "Does this add to, or diminish, the obstacles to my enlightenment?" — you will avoid the error of imagining that sins are definite acts of absolutely fixed value which can be classified, graded, and listed. They are not. What is wrong for one person may be right for another — as the Gita teaches us. Each of us has his own sins and his own virtues, relative to his duties, responsibilities and present spiritual condition. All we can do is to search our own consciences, and try to relate our motives on any particular occasion to the great central motive of our lives. Extremely difficult problems in conduct are sure to arise.

We shall make many mistakes; and the best we can hope for is that our overall intention may be in the right direction.

Patanjali teaches us to regard our sins with a certain scientific detachment which avoids the two extremes of lazy tolerance and futile disgust. The surgeon does not tolerate a cancer; he cuts it out. But he does not shrink from it in horror, either. He studies it. He tries to understand how it has grown, and how the growth of a new cancer can be prevented.

We do not sin through pure wickedness or sheer moral idiocy. Our sins have a meaning and a purpose which we shall have to understand before we can hope to stop repeating them. They are, in fact, symptoms of the pain of alienation from our real nature, the Atman. They are attempts to reunite ourselves with that nature. Such attempts are hopelessly misdirected, because they take, as their starting-point, the ignorance of egoism; they are bound to lead us farther and farther away from Reality.

We are all dimly aware of the presence of the Atman within us. We are all looking for the peace and freedom and security of perfect union with the Atman. We all long desperately to be happy. But ignorance misdirects us. It assures us that the Atman cannot really be within us, that we are nothing but individuals, separate egos. And so we start to search for this dimly conceived, eternal happiness amidst the finite and transient phenomena of the external world. Like the fabled musk deer, we search all over the earth for that haunting fragrance which is really exuded from ourselves. We stumble, we hurt ourselves, we endure endless hardships — but we never look in the right place.

The tyrant who enslaves millions of people, the miser who hoards a thousand times as much money as he could ever need, the traitor who sells his dearest friend, the murderer, the thief, the liar and the addict — all these, in the last analysis, simply want to be safe and happy and at peace. We seek security in the accumulation of possessions by violence or fruad, or by the destruction of our imagined enemies. We seek happiness through sense- gratification, through every kind of vanity and self-delusion. We seek peace through the intoxication of various drugs. And in all these activities we display an energy of heroic proportions. That is the tragedy of sin. It is tragically misdirected energy. With less effort, we might easily have found union with the Atman, had we not been misled by our ignorance.

Ignorance, says Patanjali, creates all the other obstacles to enlightenment: (More will be said about them in commenting on the next aphorisms.) They are the samskaras, the powerful tendencies which have already been referred to (chapter I, aphorism 2). These tendencies drive us to perform ever-recurring acts of sin, or obstacle-building; and so the obstacles grow automatically, through the power of desire, pride, rage and fear. The Gita describes this process:

> Thinking about sense-objects,
> Will attach you to sense-objects;
> Grow attached, and you become addicted;
> Thwart your addiction, it turns to anger;
> Be angry, and you confuse your mind;
> Confuse your mind, you forget the lesson of experience;
> Forget experience, you lose discrimination;
> Lose discrimination, and you miss life's only purpose.

The obstacles are present, to some degree, in the minds of all who have not actually attained the highest samadhi, complete union with the Atman. Patanjali lists four conditions or degrees of ignorance, as follows.

The obstacles may be potential; as in the case of very young children, whose already-existing tendencies will only manifest themselves in later life. This is said to be true also of those yogis who fail to concentrate with non-attachment and therefore become merged in the forces of Nature (chapter I, aphorism 19). When they return, as they finally must, to mortal life, they will be confronted by those obstacles which caused their original failure.

Then there are spiritual aspirants, whose minds still contain obstacles to enlightenment, but only in a vestigial form. Their samskaras continue to operate by the momentum of past karmas, but the power of these samskaras is greatly diminished, and they do not present any serious danger, as long as the aspirant is on his guard against them.

Then, again, the obstacles — or at least one group of them — may have been temporarily overcome through the cultivation of ignorance-eclipsing thoughts and virtues. If we persevere in cultivating such thoughts and virtues, we shall gradually reduce the obstacles to the vestigial form which has just been described.

Finally, the obstacles may be present in a fully developed form. This is the normal, tragic condition of all ordinary worldly minded people.

अनित्याशुचि-दुःखानात्मसु नित्य शुचि
सुखात्मख्यातिरविद्या ॥ ५ ॥

5. To regard the non-eternal as eternal, the impure as pure, the painful as pleasant and the non-Atman as the Atman—this is ignorance.

दृग्दर्शनशक्त्योरेकात्मतैवास्मिता ॥ ६ ॥

6. To identify consciousness with that which merely reflects consciousness—this is egoism.

Ignorance, by Patanjali's definition, is false indentification. It is a misunderstanding of one's real nature. If you say, "I am this body, which is named Patanjali," you are regarding the non-Atman as the Atman. And this initial act of ignorance will lead, automatically and instantaneously, to millions of similar acts. By denying the Atman within us, we deny it everywhere. We misread Nature. We dwell on the outwardness of things, and see the universe as multiplicity, not unity.

Pure, eternal joy and peace are to be found only in union with the Atman. Our ignorance debars us from that union, but the dim, confused longing for happiness remains. So we are driven to seek it in the external world. We are forced to accpet wretched substitutes and to try to persuade ourselves that they are genuine and valid. Instead of eternity, we cling to what seems relatively enduring. Instead of purity, we value what seems relatively pure. Instead of true happiness we clutch at what seems temporarily pleasant. But, also, our satisfaction is short-lived. The strongest tower falls, the most beautiful flower withers in our hands, the clearest water turns brackish and foul. Ignorance has betrayed us, as it always must. Yet, as we turn sadly away, our eyes fall upon some new object of sense attachment and desire. And so the hopeless search goes on.

The central act of ignorance is the identification of the Atman, which is consciousness itself, with the mind-body — "that which merely reflects consciousness." This is what Patanjali defines as egoism.

"At whose behest does the mind think?" asks the Kena Upanishad: "Who bids the body live? Who makes the tongue speak? Who is that effulgent Being that directs the eye to form and colour and the ear to sound? The Atman is the ear of the ear, mind of the mind, speech of the speech. He is also breath of the breath and eye of the eye. Having given up the false identification of the Atman with the senses and the mind, and knowing the Atman to be Brahman, the wise become immortal."

Western philosophy produced two schools of thought with regard to the problem of consciousness — the materialist and the idealist. The materialists believed that consciousness is a product in a process; that it arises when certain conditions are fulfilled and is lost when these conditions do not exist. Thus, according to the materialist philosophers, consciousness is not the property of any single substance. The idealist, on the other hand, believed that consciousness is the property of the mind, and were therefore faced with the conclusion that it must cease whenever the mind becomes unconscious.

Modern scientists would seem inclined to reject both these hypotheses, and to believe that consciousness is always present everywhere in the universe, even though its presence cannot always be detected scientific methods. In this, they approach the viewpoint of Vedanta. And indeed there are some distinguished scientists and scientific writers whose thinking has brought them to a study of Hindu philosophy. For example, Erwin Schrodinger in his book *What Is Life?* writes as follows:

> Consciousness is never experienced in the plural, only in the singular..... How does the idea of plurality (so emphatically opposed by the Upanishad writers) arise at all? Consciousness finds itself intimately connected with, and depedent on, the physical state of the limited region of matter, the body.... Now, there is a great plurality of similar bodies. Hence the pluralization of consciousness or minds seems a very suggestive hypothesis. Probably all simple ingenuous people, as well as the great majority of western philosophers, have accepted it....The only possible alternative is simply to keep the immediate experience that

consciousness is a singular of which the plural is unknown.; that there is only one thing and that, what seems to be a plurality, is merely a series of different aspects of this one thing, produced by a deception (the Indian Maya); the same illusion is produced in a gallery of mirrors, and in the same way Gaurisankar and Mt. Everest turned out to be the same peak seen from different valleys....

Yet each of us has the undisputable impression that the sum total of his experience and memory forms a unit, quite distinct from that of any other person. He refers to it as 'I.' *What is this 'I'?*

If you analyze it closely you will, I think, find that it is just a little bit more than a collection of single data (experiences and memories), namely the canvas *upon which* they are collected. And you will, on close introspection, find that, what you really mean by 'I', is that ground-stuff upon which they are collected. You may come to a distant country, lose sight of all your friends, may all but forget them; you acquire new friends, you share life with them as intensely as you ever did with your old ones. Less and less important will become the fact that, while living your new life, you still recollect the old one. 'The youth that was I' you may come to speak of him in the third person, indeed the protagonist of the novel you are reading is probably nearer to your heart, certainly more intensely alive and better known to you. Yet there has been no intermediate break, no death. And even if a skilled hypnotist succeeded in blotting out entirely all your earlier reminiscences, you would not find that he had killed you. In no case is there a loss of personal existence to deplore.... nor will there ever be.

सुखानुशयी रागः ॥ ७ ॥

7. Attachment is that which dwells upon pleasure.

दुःखानुशयी द्वेषः ॥ ८ ॥

8. Aversion is that which dwells upon pain.

Both are obstacles to enlightenment, or even to relative knowledge of a person or object. You cannot have any impartial, dispassionate insight into the character of one to whom you are blindly attached, or whom you regard with disgusted aversion. The spiritual aspirant must not love the things of this world too much; but he must not hate them either. Aversion, also, is a form of bondage. We are tied to what we hate or fear. That is why, in our lives, the same problem, the same danger or difficulty, will present itself over and over again in various aspects, as long as we continue to resist or run away from it instead of examining and solving it.

स्वरसवाही विदुषोऽपि तथारूढोऽभिनिवेशः ॥ ९ ॥

9. The desire to cling to life is inherent both in the ignorant and in the learned. This is because the mind retains impressions of the death experience from many previous incarnations.

The doctrine of reincarnation is, of course, common to Hinduism and Buddhism; and it was entertained, though finally rejected, by early Christianity. It has already been referred to in this commentary (chapter I, aphorisms 2, 18, and 19), but now we must discuss it more fully.

Prakriti has been defined (I.17) as the effect or power of Brahman, the Reality. In other words, this illusion (in Sanskrit, *maya*) of an objective, spatio-temporal universe is projected by the Reality itself. Therefore, it follows that Prakriti and Brahman must be co-existent, and that Prakriti, like Brahman, had no beginning and will have no end. Prakriti will continue to spin the web of a universe, to draw that web into itself, to spin the web again, over and over, forever.

At the same time, within the universe, another process is at work. For it is in the nature of the individual ego-sense to struggle slowly upward toward self-realization, from the inanimate to the animate, from the vegetable to the animal, from the animal to the human, through thousands and even millions of births, deaths and rebirths. The Atman is within the stone, no less than within the man. But the stone can never know itself as the Atman so long as it remains a stone. It must evolve through higher forms until, at last, it reaches humanity, for it is only within the human mind-body that the individual ego can known its real nature, and thus be liberated from the cycle of reincarnation.

Throughout this enormous journey toward total consciousness, the individual is subject to the Law of Karma. His desires and acts regulate the speed of his progress. He builds or removes his own obstacles to enlightenment. His present state is continually being conditioned by the karmas of his past and continually productive of future karmas. Death does not interrupt this process. Neither does rebirth. The individual is merely reborn with a body, a mind, a character and social surroundings which express, as it were, the sum total of his karmic balance at that particular moment in time.

The doctrine of reincarnation is exceedingly unpalatable to many people because it makes each one of us directly responsible for his present condition. We all dislike having to face this responsibility, and some of us prefer to blame God, or our parents, or the existing political system for making us what we are. If we deny reincarnation and claim that this birth is our first, we are, in fact, disclaiming responsibility for our condition, since it then logically follows that this condition must have been ordained by God, or brought about by the influences of heredity and environment. Hence — if we have been born physically or economically underprivileged — we are provided with a permanent grievance, which permits us to spend a lifetime sulking and cursing our fate, and with a permanent excuse for all our own weaknesses and failures.

This doctrine of reincarnation, which at first seems so grim and heartless, actually implies a profoundly optimistic belief in the justice and order of the universe. If it is we — and not God, or our parents, or our fellow men — who have made our present predicament, then it is we who can change it. We have no excuse for self-pity and no reason for despair. We are not helplessly doomed. We are under mysterious prenatal curse. The "fault, dear Brutus, is not in our stars...." All we need is courage and a determination not to give up the struggle.

Sometimes the workings of the Law of Karma are quite apparent to us — in retrospect, at least. We can see, looking back over our lives, how a certain tendency in our character has produced the same situation, over and over again, under diverse circumstances. This should certainly make us suspect that karma also operates in those areas of experience which are seemingly ruled by chance. And indeed, science keeps finding new threads of cause and effect amidst life's apparent tangle. For example, the psychologists now tell us that many "accidents" are not accidental at all, but assertions of a subconscious desire to avoid some unpleasant problem, even at the cost of breaking an arm or a leg. Similarly, genuine symptoms of physical disease may appear as the direct result of an emotional tension; and not through the simple ill luck of "picking up a germ," as was previously supposed.

In the above aphorism, Patanjali not only affirms his belief in reincarnation, but also, by implication, offers a proof of it. How could we fear death so much if we had never previously experienced it?

A hen is given duck eggs to hatch, in a farmyard where there are no adult ducks. As soon as the shells are broken, the ducklings make for water and start to swim. Who taught them to do this? Certainly not the mother hen. Seeing them in the water, she clucks wildly, thinking they will all be drowned. We say that the ducklings know how to swim "by instinct." By instinct, also, we fear death.

Now, what is instinct? According to a current American dictionary, it is "an inborn pattern of activity and response common to a given biological stock." According to the yoga philosophers, it is "involved reason" — that is, experience which has become subconscious. Both definitions agree in postulating the *memory* of an experience — a memory which is either transmitted by heredity through a species, or carried by an individual through a series of births.

The hereditist would, of course, deny reincarnation. The yoga philosopher would reconcile it with heredity, saying that the individual, being compelled by his karmas to incarnate in the form of a duck, must, thereby "inherit" a duck's attributes, including the knowledge of swimming. So the word "instinct" does not help us very much, either way, towards an explanation of man's fear of death.

It may be objected also that this "proof" or reincarnation (Patanjali will advance others, later) is unsatisfactory for another reason — why should our fear of death *necessarily* depend on remembered experience? Suppose we have had no previous experience of death, doesn't this make it all the more terrifying? Is there anything more fearful than the totally unknown? "Ay, but to die," exclaims Shakespeare's Hamlet, "and go we know not where....

This, however, is not the whole of the answer. And perhaps Patanjali's proof of reincarnation through memory of the death experience may be justified after all. Consider this passage from the Brihadaranyaka Upanishad:

> There are two states for man — the state in this world, and the state in the next; there is also a third state, the state intermediate between these two, which can be likened to dream. While in the intermediate state, a man experiences both the other states, that in this world and that in next; and the manner thereof is as follows: When he dies, he lives only in the subtle body, on which are left the impressions of his past deeds, and of these impressions he is aware, illumined as they are by the light of the Atman. The pure light of the Atman affords him light. Thus it is that in the intermediate state he experiences the first state, or that of life in the world. Again, while in the intermediate state, he foresees both the evils and the blessings that will yet come to him, as these are determined by his conduct, good and bad, upon the earth, and by the character in which this conduct has resulted. Thus it is that in the intermediate state he experiences the second state, or that of life in the world to come.

The "intermediate state" is, according to this definition, a sort of lucid post-mortem interval during which an individual takes stock of himself and is compelled to review his past deeds, together with the consequences they must now inevitably produce in his next birth upon this earth or elsewhere. In the clear, relentless light of the Atman, from which he is still alienated, he sees what he has made of himself. Obviously, for the vast majority of us, this experience cannot be other than bitterly humiliating and painful. At such a moment, surely, we must feel shame, horror and remorse of an intensity never even imagined during our embodied lives.

If, therefore, we take the term "death experience" to include experience of this intermediate state between death and rebirth it is very easy to understand why a subconscious memory of it should fill us with instinctive dread — a dread even greater than that of the unknown. Only the illumined saint can be absolutely free from fear to death, because, for him, this intermediate state is no longer in prospect. Already here on earth he has "died" to the life of the senses. And, as a man grows in spirituality, his death-fear will gradually diminish. This would seem to support Patanjali's proof of reincarnation.

In any case — and whatever its origin — the desire to postpone death and cling to life is certainly one of the greatest obstacles to enlightenment. To cling to life is to cling to normal sense consciousness, thereby shunning the superconsciousness within which the Atman is known.

ते प्रतिप्रसवहेयाः सूक्ष्माः ॥ १० ॥

10. When these obstacles have been reduced to a vestigial form, they can be destroyed by resolving the mind back into its primal cause.

ध्यानहेयास्तद्वृत्तयः ॥ ११ ॥

11. In their fully developed form, they can be overcome through meditation.

It may be found simpler to consider these two aphorisms in reverse order; since the obstacles to enlightenment must first be overcome in their fully developed or gross form (see chapter II, aphorism 4). The way in which this is to be done has been likened to the washing of a piece of dirty cloth; first, the dirt must be loosened with soap, then washed away with clean water. "Soap" represents the practice of the "preliminary steps toward yoga" (austerity, study and the dedication of the fruits of one's work to God) which are discussed in the commentary on the first aphorism of this chapter. "Water" represents the practice of meditation. "Soap" and "water" are both indispensable if the "cloth" of the mind is to be properly cleansed. The one cannot be used effectively without the other.

When the obstacles in their fully developed form have been overcome, they will still exist vestigially, as tendencies (samskaras). These tendencies are only destroyed when the mind is resolved back into its cause, that is, into Prakriti, from which the mind was projected. This is, of course, the process of going into samadhi. (See chapter I, aphorisms 41-51.)

क्लेशमूलः कर्माशयो दृष्टादृष्टजन्मवेदनीयः ॥ १२ ॥

12. A man's latent tendencies have been created by his past thoughts and actions. These tendencies will bear fruits, both in this life and in lives to come.

सति मूले तद्विपाको जात्यायुर्भोगाः ॥ १३ ॥

13. So long as the cause exists, it will bear fruits—such as rebirth, a long or a short life, and the experiences of pleasure and of pain.

ते ह्लादपरितापफलाः पुण्यापुण्यहेतुत्वात् ॥ १४ ॥

14. Experiences of pleasure and of pain are the fruits of merit and demerit, respectively.

परिणामताप-संस्कारदुःखैर्गुणवृत्तिविरोधाच्च
दुःखमेव सर्वं विवेकिनः ॥ १५ ॥

15. But the man of spiritual discrimination regards all these experiences as painful. For even the enjoyment of present pleasure is painful, since we already fear its loss. Past pleasure is painful

because renewed cravings arise from the impressions it has left upon the mind. And how can any happiness be lasting if it depends only upon our moods? For these moods are constantly changing, as one or another of the ever-warring gunas seizes control of the mind.

The operations of the Law of Karma (see chapter I, aphorism 2, 18-19) and the nature and functions of the gunas (see chapter I, aphorism 17) have already been fully described. Patanjali warns us here against imagining that some of our thoughts and acts have had, and will have no consequences, just because these consequences are not apparent. Our acts have created latent tendencies which will bear fruit in due season — perhaps conditioning the span and circumstances of future lives. Acts of merit will, it is true, produce results which can be described as "plesant": but "plesant" and "painful" are only relative terms. Like "good" and "bad," "hot" and "cold," "happy," and "unhappy" they are one of the "pairs of opposites" which, in the phraseology of the Gita, form the seeming contradictions of our experience of the external world. From the standpoint of the man of spiritual discrimination, all experience is painful, insofar as it binds us to this world and renews our senses-cravings. The only true happiness is in union with the Atman. All other "happiness" is relative, temporary, and therefore false.

हेयं दुःखमनागतम् ।। १६ ।।

16. The pain which is yet to come may be avoided.

There are three kinds of karma: the karma which has already been created and stored up, so that it will bear fruit in some future life; the karma created in the past or in some previous life, which is bearing fruit at the present moment, and the karma which we are now in the process of creating by our thoughts and acts. Of these, the already existing karmas are beyond our control; we can only wait until they have worked themselves out, and accept their fruits with courage and patience. But the karmas which we are now creating — "the pain which is yet to come" — can be avoided. Not by ceasing to act — that would be impossible, even if it were desirable — but by ceasing to desire the fruits of action for oneself. If we dedicate the fruits of action to God, we shall gradually unwind the wheel of karma and thus avoid its pain.

द्रष्टृदृश्ययोः संयोगो हेयहेतुः ॥ १७ ॥

17. This pain is caused by false identification of the experiencer with the object of experience. It may be avoided.

"The experiencer" is the Atman, our real nature. "The object of experience" is the totality of the apparent world, including the mind and the senses. In reality, the Atman alone exists, "One without a second," eternally free. But by the false identification through maya, which is the mystery of our present predicament, the Atman is mistaken for the individual ego, subject to all the thought-waves which arise and trouble the mind. That is why we imagine that we are "unhappy" or "happy", "angry" or "lustful" The Gita reminds us that this is not really the case:

The illumined soul....
Thinks always: "I am doing nothing.
No matter what he sees,
Hears, touches, smells, eats....
This he knows always:
"I am not seeing, I am not hearing:

It is the senses that see and hear
And touch the things of the senses."

So long as the experiencer is falsely identified with the object of experience, we cannot know the Atman, our real nature. We remain in bondage, believing ourselves to be the slaves of experience.

"There is a story," writes Swami Vivekananda, "that the king of the gods, Indra, once became a pig, wallowing in mire; he had a she-pig, and a lot of baby pigs, and was very happy. Then some gods saw his plight, and came to him, and told him, 'You are king of the gods, you have all the gods under your command. Why are you here?' But Indra said, 'Never mind; I am all right here; I do not care for heaven, while I have this sow and these little pigs.' The poor gods were at their wits' end. After a time, they decided to slay all the pigs, one after another. When all were dead, Indra began to weep and mourn. Then the gods ripped his pig-body open and he came out of it, and began to laugh when he realized what a hideous dream he had had; he, the king of the gods, to have become a pig, and to think that pig-life was the life? Not only so, but to have wanted the whole universe to come into the pig-life! The Atman, when it identifies itself with nature, forgets that it is pure and infinite. The Atman does not love, it is love itself. It does not exist it is existence itself. The Atman does not know; it is knowledge itself. It is a mistake to say that the Atman loves, exists or knows. Love, existence and knowledge are not the qualities of the Atman, but its essence. When they get reflected upon something, you may call them the qualities of that something. They are not the qualities but the essence of the Atman, the Infinite Being, without birth or death, established in its own glory. It appears to have become so degenerate that if you approach to tell it, 'You are not a pig,' it begins to squeal and bite."

The pig-which-is-not-a-pig can, on occasion, become a very dangerous animal. The power of tamas in our nature is so great that we hate to be disturbed. We loathe any new idea, especially if it implies that we shall have to make some change in our own lives. And so, when the spiritual teachers come to tell us that we are not pigs but God, we are quite apt to persecute and crucify them.

प्रकाश-क्रिया-स्थितिशीलं भूतेन्द्रियात्मकं
भोगापवर्गार्थं दृश्यम् ॥ १८ ॥

18. The object of experience is composed of the three gunas—the principles of illumination (sattwa), activity (rajas) and inertia (tamas). From these, the whole universe has evolved together with the instruments of knowledge—such as the mind, senses, etc.—and the objects perceived—such as the physical elements. The universe exists in order that the experiencer may experience it, and thus become liberated.

The last sentence of this aphorism is one of the most important in the entire book. It is Patanjali's answer to the pig-people; to those who want to stay wallowing in their mire.

When told that all sense-experience is, in the last analysis, painful, the pig-people become scornful and angry. They find such a philosophy cowardly and lacking in spirit. One should not be afraid of pleasure, they exclaim; one should seize the flying moment and enjoy it, whatever the consequences. They quote approvingly from their poets (for many of the finest poets write pig-poetry) saying that "one crowded hour of glorious life is worth an age without a name," and Patanjali is a timid old kill-joy grandmother.

To this accusation, Patanjali replies: "It is you who are really afraid. It is you who shrink from experience. You talk so much about your pleasures, yet you know nothing about pleasure. You never try to understand its nature. The universe of sense-experience is a great book; and he who reads it through to the end with discrimination will know at length that there is nothing but the Atman. No experience is in vain, no page of that book is superfluous, provided that the reader learns something from it and passes on to the next. But you never learn. You never pass on. You read the same page over and over, repeating the same meaningless experience, like a man who is half asleep, reading without remembering a word."

There is an Indian saying: "The bee came to suck the honey, but his feet got stuck in it." We can only avoid the fate of the bee if we regard our lives as a perpetual search for meaning, an exercise in discrimination between the real and the unreal. In that spirit, we shall welcome all kinds of experience, both pleasant and painful, and it will never harm us. For the Truth lies hidden everywhere, within every experience and every object of the universe. Everything that happens to us, no matter how seemingly trivial, throughout the day, offers some tiny clue which could lead us toward wider spiritual knowledge and eventual liberation.

विशेषाविशेष-लिङ्गमात्रालिङ्गानि गुणपर्वाणि ॥ १९ ॥

19. The gunas pass through four states—gross, subtle, primal and unevolved.

Here Patanjali summarizes what has already been explained in the commentary on aphorism 17 of the first chapter. When the universe exists only in its potential form, the gunas are in perfect equilibrium and their state is described as unevolved or "signless." When the universe begins to evolve, and the guna-balance is disturbed, we find the dawning of mahat, the cosmic ego-sense. This state is described as primal or "indicated." In the next stage of evolution, when the gunas have entered into the combinations which form the mind and the inner essences of things, their state is described as subtle or "undefined." And finally, when the universe has reached its external, physical manifestation, the state of the gunas is described gross of "defined." (Because of the difficulty of rendering these technical terms into English, an alternative translation has been given in each case.)

द्रष्टा दृशिमात्रः शुद्धोऽपि प्रत्ययानुपश्यः ॥ २० ॥

20. The Atman—the experiencer—is pure consciousness. It appears to take on the changing colors of the mind. In reality, it is unchangeable.

तदर्थ एव दृश्यस्यात्मा ॥ २१ ॥

21. The object of experience exists only to serve the purpose of the Atman.

कृतार्थं प्रति नष्टमप्यनष्टं तदन्यसाधारणत्वात् ॥ २२ ॥

22. Though the object of experience becomes unreal to him who has reached the state of liberation, it remains real to all other beings.

स्वस्वामिशक्त्योः स्वरूपोपलब्धिहेतुः संयोगः ॥ २३ ॥

23. The Atman—the experiencer—is identified with Prakriti—the object of experience—in order that the true nature of both Prakriti and Atman may be known.

तस्य हेतुरविद्या ॥ २४ ॥

24. This identification is caused by ignorance.

तदभावात् संयोगाभावो हानं तद्दृशेः
कैवल्यम् ॥ २५ ॥

25. When ignorance has been destroyed, this identification ceases. Then bondage is at an end and the experiencer is indepedent and free.

These aphorisms would seem, at first sight, to express a paradoxical idea. When Patanjali says that the experiencer is identified with the object of experience in *order* that the true nature of both may be known, and then adds that this identification is caused by ignorance — we feel a certain bewilderment. We are bewildered because Patanjali seems to be accepting and even somehow approving of this ignorance. Surely, ignorance is undesirable? Surely, it would have been much better if we had never become alienated from the Atman, never ceased to be aware of our real nature? It is rather as if a prisoner would say complacently: "This prison exists in order that I may eventually get out of it," disregarding the fact that, if he had not committed a crime, he need never have gone to prison at all.

And yet, this bewilderment that we feel is merely another product of this same ignorance. Rooted in maya, we cannot hope to understand maya or to judge the "justice" or "injustice" of its bondage by our little relative, ethical standards. All we do know for certain is this: that the great saints who found liberation did not look back upon their struggles with bitterness or regret. They did not even regard maya with horror; rather, they saw it as a fascinating and amusing play. They rejoiced in their long fight for freedom. Swami Vivekananda, near the end of his life, could write; "I am glad I was born, glad I suffered so, glad I did make big blunders, glad to enter peace." Faced by the seeming paradox of the Atman-Prakriti relationship, we are naturally troubled by doubt and confusion. But, instead of wasting our time reasoning and philosophizing, we shall do better to keep our eyes fixed on those tremendous figures who reached the end of the journey and stand, as it were, beckoning to us to follow them. Their triumph is our reassurance that somehow — in some way which we cannot yet understand — all is for the best.

विवेकख्यातिरविप्लवा हानोपाय: ॥ २६ ॥

26. Ignorance is destroyed by awakening to knowledge of the Atman, until no trace of illusion remains.

तस्य सप्तधा प्रान्तभूमि: प्रज्ञा ॥ २७ ॥

27. The experiencer gains this knowledge in seven stages, advancing toward the highest.

The seven stages by which perfect knowledge of the Atman is gained are said to be as follows:

a. The realisation that the source of all spiritual wisdom is inside ourselves; that the Kingdom of Heaven is within us. As Swami Vivekananda says: "After long searches here and there, in temples and in churches, in earths and in heavens, at last you come back, completing the circle from where you started, to your own soul and find that He, for whom you have been seeking all over the world, for whom you have been weeping and praying in churches and temples, on whom you were looking as the mystery of all mysteries shrouded in the clouds, is nearest of the near, is your own Self, the reality of your life, body and soul."

These are stirring words, to which our hearts can immediately respond; but a firm realization of their truth is not so easily achieved. It is not enough to accept it as an intellectual proposition. It is not enough to glimpse it in moments of religious emotion or temporary insight. We cannot claim to have reached this first stage until we are continuously aware of the presence of the Atman within us. When we are aware of this, we know also, without any doubt, that union with the Atman is possible, since no external obstacles can arise to prevent it.

b. The cessation of pain. Pain, as we have seen, is caused by our attachment or aversion to the phenomena of the external universe. As the mind turns inward toward knowledge of the Atman, these attachments and aversions lose their power. We have already quoted the Gita's phrase: "Yoga is the breaking of contact with pain."

c. Samadhi — complete realization of, and union with the Atman. The objective universe disappears. The Atman is experienced as total existence, consciousness and joy. In this experience, all sense of individual separateness and differentiation is lost. In Shankara's *Crest-Jewel of Discrimination*, the Disciple who has reached samadhi exclaims: "My mind fell like a hailstone into that vast expanse of Brahman's ocean. Touching one drop of it, I melted away and became one with Brahman. And now, though I return to human consciousness, I abide in the joy of the Atman. Where is this universe? Who took it away? Has it merged into something else? A while ago, I beheld it — now it exists no longer. This is wonderful indeed! Here is the ocean of Brahman, full of endless joy. How can I accept or reject anything? Is there anything apart or distinct from Brahman? Now, finally and clearly, I know that I am the Atman, whose nature is eternal joy. I see nothing, I hear nothing, I know nothing that is separate from me."

d. When a man comes out of samadhi, he returns to consciousness of the objective universe; but this consciousness differs from the kind which we all experience. To one who has achieved samadhi, the external world is known to be merely an appearance. In Shankara's phrase, "it is and is not." The man of illumination no longer identifies the external world with the Atman. He sees that it is only a reflection of the Atman — not, indeed, utterly unreal, since it is projected by the Reality; yet lacking substance and independent existence, like an image in a mirror.

In this stage, a man knows that he is no longer bound by any worldly duty or obligation. "His acts", as the Gita puts it, "fall from him." This does not, of course, mean that a man who has achieved samadhi will thence- forward do nothing at all. On the contrary, most of the great saints have been very active, particularly in teaching others. "They are like big steamships," said Sri Ramakrishna, "which not only cross the ocean themselves but carry many passengers to the other shore." But the actions of the illumined saint differ from the actions of ordinary men, because they are not motivated by any attachment or selfish desire. They are, in the most literal sense of the word, voluntary action. Action, for the rest of us, is only partially voluntary; it always contains an element of compulsion due to our past karmas and present involvements in the life of the senses. For this reason, the behaviour of a saint is often very hard for us to understand; it seems strange, arbitrary or capricious, precisely because it is not subject to our familiar compulsions. A great teacher was once asked to explain one of the most seemingly mysterious actions recorded in the Gospels, Christ's cursing of a barren fig tree. "Become a Christ," he replied smilingly, "and then you will know why he did that."

e. Next comes the realization that the mind and the objective world have both ended their services to the experiencer. The mind has been the instrument, and the world the object of the experience whereby the experiencer has come to know the Atman, his real nature. The mind has been used to transcend the mind, just as we use a ladder to "transcend" a ladder. Once we have reached the sill of the window against which it rested, the ladder can be kicked away; we do not need it any more.

f. Now the stored-up impressions within the mind, and the gunas themselves, fall away forever, "like rocks," (to quote one of the classical commentators) "fallen from the top of the mountain peak, never to return."

g. And so the final stage is reached — the state of eternal existence in union with the Atman. Now there is no more returning from samadhi to partial sense-consciousness, no more identification with the mind. We realize, in the words of Vivekananda, "that we have been alone throughout the universe, neither body nor mind was ever related, much less joined, to us. They were working their own way, and we, through ignorance, joined ourselves to them. But we have been alone, omnipotent, omnipresent, ever blessed; our own Atman was so pure and perfect that we required nothing else; throughout the universe there can be nothing that will not become effulgent before our knowledge. This will be the last state, and the Yogi will become peaceful and calm, never to feel any more pain, never to be again deluded, never to be touched by misery. He will know that he is ever blessed, ever perfect, almighty."

योगाङ्गानुष्ठानादशुद्धिक्षये ज्ञानदीप्तिरा-
विवेकख्यातेः ॥ २८ ॥

28. As soon as all impurities have been removed by the practice of spiritual disciplines—the "limbs" of yoga— a man's spiritual vision opens to the light-giving knowledge of the Atman.

Patanjali now begins a detailed description of the so-called "limbs" of yoga — the various rules and practices which we must observe in order to clear the mind of its impurities. To remove these impurities — the obstacles to knowledge of the Atman — is the sole purpose of spiritual disciplines. For the knowledge itself does not have to be sought. It is already within us — unlike that mundane knowledge which must be acquired from books and experiences in the external world. When the obstacles have been removed, the ever-present Atman is immediately revealed.

यम-नियमासन-प्राणायाम-प्रत्याहार-धारणा-ध्यान-
समाधयोऽष्टावङ्गानि ॥ २९ ॥

29. The eight limbs of yoga are: the various forms of abstention from evil-doing (yama), the various observances (niyamas), posture (asana), control of the prana (pranayama), withdrawal of the mind from sense objects (pratyahara), concentration

(dharana), meditation (dhyana) and absorption in the Atman (samadhi).

अहिंसा-सत्यास्तेय-ब्रह्मचर्यापरिग्रहा यमाः ॥ ३० ॥

30. Yama is abstention from harming others, from false-hood, from theft, from incontinence, and from greed.

We are to live so that no harm or pain is caused by our thoughts, words or deeds to any other being. In a positive sense, this means that we must cultivate love for all, and try to see the one Atman within everybody. We must think of ourselves as the servants of mankind, and be ready to put ourselves at the disposal of those who need us. It does not mean, however, that we should lend ourselves to the evil purposes of others, helping them to commit crimes; for such purposes would be in opposition to the ideals of *yama.* The truly helpful man is like a public trolley car, available to all who care to use it, but travelling, nevertheless, along a fixed route to its destination.

Our words and our thoughts must be truthful, always in conformity with the facts. Sri Ramakrishna used to say that true spirituality consists in "making the heart and the lips the same." But we must be careful not to hurt others by saying what is cruel, even if it happens to be true. On such occasions we have to remain silent.

It is not enough simply to abstain from theft; we must not harbour any feelings of covetousness, either toward persons or objects. We must remember that nothing in this world really belongs to us. At best, we are merely borrowers. It is our duty, therefore, to borrow no more from the world than we absolutely need, and to make full and proper use of it Taking more than we need, and wasting it, is a form of stealing from the rest of mankind.

Continence is chastity in word, thought and deed. To be freed from the idea of sex is to achieve purity of heart. Sex is inseparable from attachment, attachment is an obstacle to spiritual knowledge.

Abstention from greed has also been interpreted as abstention from receiving gifts. To quote Swami Vivekananda: "The mind of the man who receives gifts is acted upon by the mind of the giver, so the receiver is likely to become degenerated. Receiving gifts is prone to destroy the independence of the mind, and make us slavish." This may seem to many of us to be "a hard saying"; but we must remember that Patanjali is describing the strict disciplines of the dedicated yogi. In the everyday world, most gifts can be be regarded as relatively harmless, as long as they are tokens of genuine affection. Nevertheless, there are some which are not — especially when they belong to that rather sinister category described by incometax specialists as "business gifts" — and we must beware, in general, of a too easy acceptance of other people's generosity and hospitality.

एते जाति-देश-काल-समयानवच्छिन्ना:
सार्वभौमा महाव्रतम् ॥ ३१ ॥

31. These forms of abstention are basic rules of conduct. They must be practised without any reservations as to time, place, purpose, or caste rules.

Patanjali admits of no excuses or exceptions. When he tells us, for example, to abstain from harming other he means exactly what he says. He would have no patience with a man who assured him: "Certainly I'll abstain from killing — except, of course, in time of war, on a battlefield, when we're fighting in a just cause and it's my duty anyway, as a member of the armed forces."

शौच-सन्तोष-तपः स्वाध्यायेश्वरप्रणिधानानि नियमाः ॥ ३२ ॥

32. The niyamas (observances) are purity, contentment, mortification, study and devotion to God.

Purity is cleanliness, both physical and mental. If a man thinks of himself as being the dwelling-place of the Atman, he will naturally feel that his body and mind have to be kept clean. External cleanliness is chiefly important because of its psychological effect upon us; the mere act of washing suggests the removal of mental as well as physical dirt. After a good bath, we are apt to say involuntarily: "Ah, now I feel better!"

The internal organs of the body must be cleansed and strengthened by following a proper diet. Similarly, we must follow a mental "diet" in order to cleanse and strengthen the mind. We must regulate our reading, our conversation, and indeed, our whole intake of mental "food." We must cultivate the society of those who are spiritual minded. This does not, of course, involve an absolute taboo on certain persons and topics, on the grounds that they are "worldly" or "sinful." Such negative puritanism would only lead to self-righteous pride and a furtive desire for what was forbidden. What really matters, as always, is our own attitude. If we never relax in the exercise of discrimination, we shall find that every human encounter, everything that we read or are told, has something to teach us. But this discriminative awareness is very hard to maintain, and so the beginner has to be careful. The danger in gossip, "light" entertainment, ephemeral journalism, popular fiction, radio-romancing, etc., is simply this: they encourage us to drift into a relaxed reverie, neutral at first but soon coloured by anxieties, addictions and aversions, so that the mind becomes dark and impure. Cleanliness of mind can only be maintained by constant alertness. "Once thrown off its balance," said St. Francois de Sales, "the heart is no longer its own master."

A Hindu teacher tells us: "Always talk to everyone about God." This is subtle and profound advice. For talking about God does not merely include the discussion of overtly "religious" topics. Almost any topic, no matter how seemingly "worldly," can be considered in relation to the underlying spiritual reality. It is not so much *what* we talk about as *how* we talk about it, that matters. Nor is it necessary to use such words as "God," "spirit," "prayer." etc. at all. These words serve to alienate unsympathetic hearers and make them feel that we are setting ourselves apart from them on a pedestal of holiness. We shall do better to remember that every human being is searching, however confusedly, for meaning in life and will welcome discussion of that meaning, provided that we can find a vocabulary which speaks to his or her condition. If we approach conversation from this angle and conduct it with charity, frankness, sincerity and a serious interest in the opinions of others, we shall be surprised to find how much tacit spiritual interchange can result from apparently casual talk about everyday events, science, art, politics or sport.

As for the other observances — we have already considered the significance of "mortification" and "study" in commenting on the first aphorism of chapter II. Contentment means contented acceptance of one's lot in life, untroubled by envy and restlessness. Since religious teachers are often accused of preaching passive acceptance of an unjust *status quo*, it is necessary, however, to remark that Patanjali is *not* telling us to be contented with the lot of others. Such "contentment" would be mere callous indifference. We have no right to reprove a starving beggar for being discontented. Rather, as members of a community, we have a positive duty to help less fortunate neighbours toward better and fairer living conditions. But our efforts in this direction will be much more effective if they are not inspired by motives of personal gain and advantage.

वितर्कबादने प्रतिपक्षभावनम् ॥ ३३ ॥

33. To be free from thoughts that distract one from yoga, thoughts of an opposite kind must be cultivated.

This is the technique of raising an opposing thought-wave in order to overcome distracting thought-waves in the mind. It has already been discussed in connection with the first five aphorisms of Chapter I.

वितर्का हिंसादयः कृतकारितानुमोदिता लोभक्रोध-
मोहपूर्वका मृदुमध्याधिमात्रा दुःखाज्ञानानन्तफला
इति प्रतिपक्षभावनम् ॥ ३४ ॥

34. The obstacles to yoga—such as acts of violence and untruth—may be directly created or indirectly caused or approved, they may be motivated by greed, anger or self-interest, they may be small or moderate or great, but they never cease to result in pain and ignorance. One should

overcome distracting thoughts by remembering this.

Everything we do, say, or think, or even indirectly cause or passively sanction, will inevitably produce consequences — good, bad, or composite — and these consequences will react in some measure upon ourselves. Our most secret ill-wishes toward others, our remotest permission of evil done to others, can only end by hurting us by increasing our own ignorance and pain. This is an absolute law of Nature. If we could remember it always, we should learn to control our tongues and our thoughts.

अहिंसाप्रतिष्ठायां तत्सन्निधौ वैरत्यागः ॥ ३५ ॥

35. **When a man becomes steadfast in his abstention from harming others, then all living creatures will cease to feel enmity in his presence.**

We are accustomed to use the word "harmless" in a rather derogatory sense; it has become almost synonymous with "ineffectual." Yet the perfected harmlessness of the saint is by no means ineffectual — it has a positive psychological force of tremendous power. When a man has truly and entirely renounced violence in his own thoughts and in his dealings with others, he begins to create an atmosphere around himself within which violence and enmity must cease to exist because they find no reciprocation. Animals, too, are sensitive to such an atmosphere. Wild beasts may be temporarily cowed with whips, but they can only be rendered harmless by the power of genuine harmlessness, as every good trainer knows. A lady who was accustomed to handle deadly snakes used to explain: "You see, they know I won't hurt them."

"The test of *ahimsa* (harmlessness) is absence of jealousy," said Swami Vivekananda. "The so-called great men of the world may all be seen to become jealous of each other for a small name, for a little fame, and for a few bits of gold. So long as this jealousy exists in a heart, it is far away from the perfection of ahimsa."

सत्यप्रतिष्ठायां क्रियाफलाश्रयत्वम् ।। ३६ ।।

36. When a man becomes steadfast in his abstention from falsehood he gets the power of obtaining for himself and others the fruits of good deeds, without having to perform the deeds themselves.

An ordinary man is said to be truthful when his words correspond to the facts of which he speaks. But when a man becomes perfected in truthfulness, he gains control, so to speak, of the truth. He no longer has to "obey" facts; facts obey him. He cannot think or even dream a lie; everything he says become true. If he blesses someone, that person *is* blessed — no matter whether the blessing was deserved or not. He has, in other words, the power of conferring "the fruits of good deeds" in a manner which is not subject to the Law of Karma. He can also perform miraculous cures by simply telling the sick man that he is well.

अस्तेयप्रतिष्ठायां सर्वरत्नोपस्थानम् ।। ३७ ।।

37. When a man becomes steadfast in his abstention from theft, all wealth comes to him.

This aphorism can be explained in two ways. In the first place, when a man becomes free from all feelings of covetousness he no longer experiences the lack of anything; he is therefore in the same situation as the richest man on earth. Secondly, it is true that a lack of desire for material benefits actually seems, in many cases, to attract those benefits. As Vivekananda puts it: "The more you fly from nature the more she follows you, and if you do not care for her at all she becomes your slave."

ब्रह्मचर्यप्रतिष्ठायां वीर्यलाभः ॥ ३८ ॥

38. When a man becomes steadfast in his abstention from incontinence, he acquires spiritual energy.

Sexual activity, and the thoughts and fantasies of sex, use up a great portion of our vital force. When that force is conserved through abstinence, it becomes sublimated as spiritual energy. Such energy is indispensable to a spiritual teacher; it is the power by which he transmits understanding to his pupils. For true religion is not "taught," like history or mathematics; it is transmitted, like light or heat.

अपरिग्रहस्थैर्ये जन्मकथन्तासंबोधः ॥ ३९ ॥

39. When a man becomes steadfast in his abstention from greed, he gains knowledge of his past, present and future existences.

Attachment, and the anxiety which accompanies attachment, are obstacles to knowledge. As long as you are clinging desperately to the face of a precipice (and thereby to your life) you are in no condition to survey the place you climbed up from or the place toward which you are climbing. So Patanjali tells us that freedom from attachment will result in knowledge of the whole course of our human journey, through past and future existences. Such knowledge, would, of course, be in itself a proof of the theory of reincarnation.

शौचात्स्वाङ्गजुगुप्सा परैरसंसर्गः ॥ ४० ॥

40. As the result of purity, there arises indifference

toward the body and disgust for physical intercourse with others.

सत्त्वशुद्धि-सौमनस्यैकाग्र्येन्द्रियजयात्मदर्शन-
योग्यत्वानि च ॥ ४१ ॥

41. Moreover, one achieves purification of the heart, cheerfulness of mind, the power of concentration, control of the passions and fitness for vision of the Atman.

Patanjali now describes the results which are obtained by practising the various observances (*niyamas*).

The physical body is the grossest and most outward manifestation of our consciousness. As a man's mind becomes purified, he naturally loses his sense of identification with his body. Therefore he grows indifferent to it, regarding it as a mere external garment which is neither new nor clean. Furthermore, he ceases to desire the bodies of others, since he no longer identifies those bodies with the consciousness that inhabits them. If we really knew and loved the Atman within others, the sexual act would seem utterly meaningless to us. When the Atman is known to be everywhere and always a unity, why should two outer coverings embrace?

Purity of mind shows itself in a man's mood. He becomes increasingly dominated by sattwa, the guna of illumination and peaceful happiness. "The first sign of your becoming religious," says Vivekananda, "is that you are becoming cheerful. To the yogi, everything is bliss, every human face that he sees brings cheerfulness to him. Misery is caused by sin, and by no other cause. What business have you with clouded faces? If you have a clouded face do not go out that day, shut yourself up in your room. What right have you to carry this disease out into the world?"

सन्तोषादनुत्तमः सुखलाभः ॥४२॥

42. As the result of contentment, one gains supreme happiness.

It is well worth analyzing the circumstances of those occasions on which we have been truly happy. For, as John Masefield says, "The davs that make us happy make us wise." When we review them, we shall almost certainly find that they had one characteristic in common. There were times when, for this or that reason, we had temporarily ceased to feel anxious; when we lived — as we so seldom do — in the depths of the present moment, without regretting the past or worrying about the future. This is what Patanjali means by contentment.

.There is also, of course, the happiness which comes from the satisfaction of a desire. This can be very vivid, but it is limited by its own nature to a comparatively short duration. For the satisfaction of one desire immediately gives rise to another, and so the moment of happiness ends in further anxiety. And even the satisfaction itself has, as it were, an ever-present shadow behind it. Marcel Proust, writing about sexual love, says that it contains "a permanent strain of suffering which happiness neutralizes, but which may at any moment become what it would long since have been had we not obtained what we were seeking, sheer agony." This unpleasant truth becomes very apparent in retrospect. And if you compare your memories, you will usually find that the moments of satisfaction have grown dim and confused, while the moments of contentment have remained through many years.

Logically, there is no reason why contentment should cause happiness. One might — if one had never experienced it — reasonably suppose that an absence of desire would merely produce a dull, neutral mood, equally joyless and sorrowless. The fact that this is not so is striking proof that intense happiness, the joy of the Atman, is always within us; that it can be released at any time by breaking down the barriers of desire and fear which we have built around it. How, otherwise, could we be so happy without any apparent reason?

कायेन्द्रियसिद्धिरशुद्धिक्षयात्तपसः ॥ ४३ ॥

43. As the result of mortification, impurities are removed. Then special powers come to the body and the senseorgans.

The practice of self-discipline refines our sense-perceptions and even our physical substance until we become aware of latent psychic powers, such as the power of clairvoyance, telepathy, levitation, etc.

स्वाध्यायादिष्टदेवतासम्प्रयोगः ॥ ४४ ॥

44. As the result of study, one obtains the vision of that aspect of God which one has chosen to worship.

As we have already noted (chapter II, aphorism I), Patanjali means by "study" not only the reading of the scriptures but also the practice of making japam, that is, repeating the mantram (the holy name of a chosen aspect of God) which your teacher has given you at the time of your initiation (I, 27-29). It is to the practice of japam that Patanjali here specifically refers.

समाधिसिद्धिरीश्वरप्रणिधानात् ॥ ४५ ॥

45. As the result of devotion to God, one achieves samadhi.

This, and the preceding aphorism, both refer to what is called *bhakti yoga.* We have already mentioned these yogas, or paths to union with God. Now, for the sake of clarity, it will be well to define the four which are most important.

Bhakti yoga is the path of loving devotion to God. It is expressed by means of ritual worship, prayer and japam. It is the cultivation of a direct, intense personal relationship between worshiper and worshiped. In the practice of bhakti yoga, some special aspect of God, or some divine incarnation, is chosen, so that the devotee's love may become more easily concentrated. For those who are naturally drawn to this approach, it is probably the simplest of all. And there is no doubt that the great majority of believers, in all the world's major religions, are fundamentally bhakti yogis.

Karma yoga is the path of selfless, God-dedicated action. By dedicating the fruits of one's work to God, and by working always with right means toward right ends (to the best of one's knowledge and ability at any particular moment), one may gradually achieve wisdom and non-attachment. Action is transcended through action. The bonds of attachment fall away. The wheel of karma ceases to revolve. Peace comes to the spirit. And Brahman is known. Karma yoga is the path best suited to vigorous temperaments which feel the call to duty and service in the world of human affairs. It leads such people through the dangers of overeagerness and undue anxiety and shows them how to find "the inaction that is within action," the calm in the midst of the turmoil. Sri Krishna's advice to Arjuna in the Gita is largely concerned with the practice of karma yoga.

Jnana yoga is the path of intellectual discrimination, the way of finding Brahman through analysis of the real nature of phenomena. The jnana yogi rejects all that is transient and apparent and superficial, saying "not this, not this," and so comes to length to Brahman by the process of elimination. This is a difficult path, calling for tremendous powers of will and clarity of mind. It is not for ordinary people. But it has attracted and made saints of many remarkable men and women who would otherwise not have embraced religion in any form.

Raja yoga is often called the yoga of meditation. It is not so easy to define as the other yogas, since, in a sense, it combines all of them. For meditation may include God-dedicated action (i.e., ritual worship), discrimination and concentration upon a chosen aspect of God. Raja yoga is also concerned with the study of the body as a vehicle of spiritual energy. It describes, for example, the nature and function of the various psychic centers, such as the "lotus of the heart," already referred to (chapter I, aphorism 36). Since raja yoga stresses the value of formal, scientific meditation, it is primarily for those who desire to lead monastic, or at least predominantly contemplative lives. But it should certainly be studied by every spiritually minded person. It teaches us the importance of technique in prayer.

Needless to say, these categories should not be too strictly applied, to distinguish between the varieties of spiritual temperament. One yoga cannot be practiced to the entire exclusion of the others. No one who follows a truly religious path can do so without love, discrimination and dedicated action. No one can dispense with meditation altogether. Love without discrimination lapses into sentimentality. Discrimination without love leads to spiritual pride. And we are all involved in action, "like fire in smoke." Christianity, for example, is pre-eminently a bhakti approach to God, yet among its saints we find such jnana types as Thomas Aquinas and such karma yogis as Vincent de Paul.

It is all a matter of emphasis; and, in the last analysis, each one of us has his or her own particular blend of yogas. But the observance of the "limbs of yoga" is essential, no matter which yoga one follows.

On the subject of bhakti yoga, it is worth quoting a recorded conversation between Sri Ramakrishna and one of his pupils.

> Pupil: "Sir, is God with form or is he formless?"
>
> Sri Ramakrishna: "None can say with finality that he is "this' and 'nothing else.' He is formless and again he is with forms. For a devotee he assumes forms. He is formless to the jnani, who, following the path of discrimination, has experienced in his inner being the nothingness of his ego and of the world of appearance. They are like a dream. He realizes Brahman in his own inner consciousness. Words fail to express that Reality. To the devotee the world is real, a creation of God, and himself also real as a separate entity. To the devotee, God appears as a Personal Being.
>
> 'Do you know what it is like? Compare Brahman to an ocean that is shoreless. Through the cooling influence, as it were, of the devotee's intense love, the formless water has frozen, at places, into ice blocks. That is to say, God sometimes reveals himself as a Person and with forms to his devotees. Again, with the rising of the sun of knowledge, the ice blocks melt away; then one does not see him as a Person, nor does one see his forms. Who is there then to describe whom? The ego then has completely disappeared."
>
> Pupil: "Sir, why are there so many divergent opinions about the nature of God?"
>
> Sri Ramakrishna: "Really they are not contradictory. As a man realizes him, so does he express himself. If somehow one attains him, then one finds no contradiction..... Kabir used to say: 'The formless Absolute is my Father, and God with form is Mother.' "
>
> Pupil: Sir, can one see God? If so, why can't we see him?

Sri Ramakrishna: Yes, he can assuredly be seen. One can see him with form, and one can see him also as formless."

Pupil: 'Then by what means can one see him?"

Sri Ramakrishna: "Can you weep for him with a yearning heart? Men shed a jugful of tears for their children or wife or money But who weeps for God? So long as the child remains engrossed with toys, the mother is busy doing household duties. When the child gets tired of its toys, throws them aside and cries for its mother, then the mother runs in haste and takes the child in her arms."

Just as the devotee may choose the particular aspect of God he feels most inclined to worship, so also he may choose the particular kind of relationship he wants to establish between God and himself. To Jesus, God was a Father. To Ramakrishna, God was a Mother. Brother Lawrence regarded himself as God's servant. The Wise Men of the East adored God as the Christ child. In the person of Sri Krishna, Arjuna saw God as a Friend, while Radha saw him as a Lover. Thus all human relationships may be sublimated through the practice of bhakti yoga.

स्थिरसुखमासनम् ॥ ४६ ॥

46. Posture (asana) is to be seated in a position which is firm but relaxed.

Asana means two things: the place on which the yogi sits, and the manner in which he sits there. With regard to the first meaning, the Gita tells us: "The place where he sits should be firm, neither too high nor too low, and situated in a clean spot. He should first cover it with sacred grass, then with a deerskin; then lay a cloth over these." Such were the traditional requirements; but any convenient, steady seat will do as well.

Posture, also, is defined by Hindu tradition. The most famous asana is the so-called lotus posture, in which the yogi sits cross-legged, with the feet drawn into rest against the tops of the thighs. And there are many others, requiring an even greater flexibility of the limbs. All that really matters, however, is to take up a position in which one can sit absolutely still and erect, holding the chest, neck and head in a straight line, but without strain; so that one can forget the body altogether. This is by no means easy, at first. Elderly beginners may find it best to sit upright on a chair. But it is wiser to sit on the ground because, when some degree of deep absorption has been achieved, there is always a danger of falling.

The value of holding the body erect must be apparent to those who have never practised meditation. It is a mattter of common experience that one thinks more clearly in that position than when one is sitting with a bent back. But, for the yogi, the erect posture is absolutely necessary. When the mind becomes deeply absorbed, a spiritual current is felt to rise through the spine; and the passage for this current must be kept straight and open. More will be said about this subject in commenting on aphorisms 49 and 50 of this chapter.

प्रयत्नशैथिल्यानन्तसमापत्तिभ्याम् ॥ ४७ ॥

47. Posture becomes firm and relaxed through control of the natural tendencies of the body, and through meditation on the infinite.

A good natural posture is very rare. Most people hold themselves badly and are subject to all sorts of physical tensions. Asana must therefore be perfected by careful training. The aim is to achieve an effortless alertness, in which the body is perfectly steady and yet perfectly relaxed. Since a mal-adjusted body only expresses a tense and restless state of mind, we are told to calm our minds by meditating on what is infinite. Our minds are incapable of imagining the infinite Brahman; but instead, we can think of the limitless expanse of the sky.

ततो द्वन्द्वानभिघात: ॥ ४८ ॥

48. Thereafter, one is no longer troubled by the dualities of sense-experience.

That is to say, by what the Gita calls "the pairs of opposites," the apparent dualities of the phenomenal world — such as heat and cold, pleasure and pain, good and evil, etc.

Such complete mastery of the body does not, of course, come through posture alone. It arises from a state of absorption in the consciousness of God. Patanjali goes on to describe the further practices which are necessary in order to reach this state.

तस्मिन् सति श्वासप्रश्वासयोर्गतिविच्छेद:
प्राणायाम: ॥ ४९ ॥

49. After mastering posture, one must practice control of the prana (pranayama) by stopping the motions of inhalation and exhalation.

ब्राह्याभ्यन्तरस्तम्भवृत्ति: देशकालसंख्याभि:
परिदृष्टो दीर्घ सूक्ष्म: ॥ ५० ॥

50. The breath may be stopped externally, or internally, or checked in mid-motion, and regulated according to place, time and a fixed

number of moments, so that the stoppage is either protracted or brief.

As we have seen (chapter I, aphorism 34), prana means the vital energy by which we live. Because this energy is renewed by breathing, prana may sometimes be translated as "breath", but the word has a much broader reference — for all the powers of the body and all the functions of the senses and the mind are regarded as expressions of the force of prana.

To quote the Prasna Upanishad:

"Then Bhargava approached the teacher and asked:

"Holy sir, how many several powers hold together this body? Which of them are most manifest in it? And which is the greatest?"

"The powers," replied the sage, "are ether, air, fire, water, earth—these being the five elements which compose the body; and, besides these, speech, mind, eye, ear, and the rest of the sense organs. Once these powers made the boastful assertion: "We hold the body together and support it,' whereupon Prana, the primal energy, supreme over them all, said to them. 'Do not deceive yourselves. It is I alone, dividing myself fivefold, who hold together this body and support it.' But they would not believe him.

"Prana, to justify himself, made as if he intended to leave the body. But as he rose and appeared to be going, all the rest realized that if he went they also would have to depart with him; and as Prana again seated himself, the rest found their respective places. As bees go out when their queen goes out, and return when she returns, so was it with speech, mind, vision, hearing, and the rest. Convinced of their error, the powers now praised Prana, saying:

"As fire, Prana burns; as the sun, he shines; as cloud, he rains; as Indra, he rules the gods; as wind, he blows; as the moon, he nourishes all. He is that which is visible and also that which is invisible. He is immortal life."

According to the physiology of raja yoga, a huge reserve of spiritual energy is situated at the base of the spine. This reserve of energy is known as the *kundalini*, "that which is coiled up"; hence, it is sometimes referred to as the "serpent power." When the kundalini is aroused, it is said to travel up the spine through six centres of consciousness, reaching the seventh, the center of the brain. As it reaches the higher centers, it produces various degrees of enlightenment. The process is best explained in the words of Ramakrishna.

> The scriptures speak of seven centers of consciousness. The mind may dwell in one or the other of the centers. When the mind is attached to worldliness, it dwells in the three lower centers — at the navel, the organ of reproduction, and the organ of evacuation. The mind then has no higher spiritual ambitions or visions. It is immersed in the cravings of lust and greed.
>
> The fourth center is at the heart. When the mind learns to dwell there, man experiences his first spiritual awakening. Then he has the vision of light all around. Seeing this divine light, he becomes filled with wonder and says: "Ah, how blissful!" His mind does not then run to the lower centers.
>
> The fifth center is at the throat. He whose mind has reached this center is freed from ignorance and delusion. He does not enjoy hearing or talking of anything but God.
>
> The sixth center is at the forehead. When the mind reaches this center, there is the direct vision of God, day and night. Even then, there is a little trace of ego left in the aspirant..... It is like a light in a lantern; one feels as if one could touch the light but cannot, because of the obstructing pane of glass.
>
> The seventh center is at the top of the head. When the mind reaches it, samadhi is attained. One becomes a knower of Brahman, united with Brahman.

The study of raja yoga should be very helpful to those whose minds have been warped by a conventional puritan upbringing. The danger of puritanism is that it inclines us to regard certain functions and powers of the body as evil, and other functions and powers as good, without seeing any relation between the two groups. Raja yoga reminds us that the mind-body has only one life-force. This force expresses itself in different ways at different levels of consciousness. It may impel a man to paint a picture, run a race, have sexual intercourse, or say his prayers. But it is always the same force, no matter where it takes you; just as, in a department store, the same elevator takes you to the women's hats, the sports department, the furniture, and the restaurant on the roof. Some people who have read (and misunderstood) Freud are apt to say sneeringly: "Religion is nothing but repressed sex." And this remark is supposed to shock us into giving up religion in disgust. But it would not have shocked Patanjali in the least, though he might have laughed at its stupidity. "Sex," he would have retorted, "is nothing but potential religion. Use the same energy for a higher purpose, and you will obtain enlightenment."

According to raja yoga, the spinal column contains two nerve-currents (*ida* on the left and *pingala* on the right) and a central passage which is called the *sushumna.* When the kundalini is aroused, it passes up the sushumna which, in normally unspiritual persons, remains closed. In speaking of the centers of the navel, heart, throat, etc., Ramakrishna is using physical terms to give the approximate positions of the centers, which are actually situated within the sushumna itself.

These centers are also often called "lotuses" in yogic literature, because they are said to appear in the form of a lotus to those whose spiritual vision enables them to see them. (see I, 36.) Vivekananda suggests that we may think of them as corresponding to the various plexuses of Western physiology. As we have seen, yoga physiology makes no absolute distinction between gross and subtle matter, it is all a question of degree.

"When," says Vivekananda, "by the power of long internal meditation the vast mass of energy stored up travels along the sushumna and strikes the centers, the reaction is tremendous, immensely superior to the reaction of dream or imagination, immensely more intense than the reaction of sense-perception. Wherever there was any manifestation of what is ordinarily called supernatural power or wisdom, there a little current of kundalini must have found its way into the sushumna. Only, in the vast majority of such cases, people had ignorantly stumbled on some practice which set free a minute portion of the coiled-up kundalini. All worship, consciously or unconsciously, leads to this end. The man who thinks that he is receiving response to his prayers does not know that the fulfilment comes from his own nature, that he has succeeded by the mental attitude of prayer in waking up a bit of this infinite power which is coiled up within himself. What, thus, man ignorantly worships under various names, through fear and tribulation, the yogi declares to the world to be the real power coiled up in every being, the mother of eternal happiness, if we but know how to approach her. And yoga is the science of religion, the rationale of all worship, all prayers, forms, ceremonies and miracles."

The object of pranayama is to rouse the kundalini and thereby control the prana, the vital energy. Prana, as has been said, manifests itself primarily in the function of breathing. Therefore, control of the prana may be obtained by the practice of breathing exercises.

The whole technique of pranayama is centered in the stopping of the breath. If the breath is checked after an exhalation, when the lungs have been emptied of air, the stoppage is said to be "external." If the breath is checked after an inhalation, this is an "internal" stoppage. By "place" is meant the particular part of the body at which the breath is checked — since an inhalation or exhalation need not necessarily be total. Then again, the breath may be held for a period of time.

These are highly technical matters, which have little place in this commentary, since we are chiefly concerned with Patanjali's spiritual and philosophical teaching. What must be emphasized is this: no one should practise the advanced exercises of pranayama without the constant supervision of an experienced teacher. And no one should practise them under any circumstances unless he is leading an absolutely chaste life devoted entirely to the search for God. Otherwise they may easily lead to mental disturbances of the most dangerous kind. Those who encourage others to adopt such practices out of curiosity or vanity can only be described as criminals. The tremendous power of the kundalini is not something to be lightly played with and abused.

There is, however, a harmless breathing exercise which may be used to calm the mind and prepare it for concentration. Close the right nostril with the thumb of the right hand and breathe in deeply through the left nostril. Feel, as you do so, that you are inhaling the pure and sacred prana in the life-breath and sending a current down the ida nerve to the kundalini, situated within its basic triangular lotus at the bottom of the spine. Hold the breath for a moment, repeating the sacred syllable OM. Then, as you release the right nostril, close the left nostril, with the forefinger. Exhale through the right nostril, feeling, as you do so, that you are expelling all impurities from the body.

Then, still keeping the left nostril closed, inhale through the right nostril, sending the current down the pingala nerve, and repeating the process in reverse. (In other words, only one nostril is kept open at a time, and the change is always just before exhalation.) This exercise may be continued for several minutes, until one begins to feel its calming effects. It cannot possibly do any injury, since it does not involve holding the breath excessively or over-stimulating the body with too much oxygen.

बाह्याभ्यन्तरविषयाक्षेपी चतुर्थः ॥ ५१ ॥

51. The fourth kind of pranayama is the stoppage of the breath which is caused by concentration upon external or internal objects.

The two preceding aphorisms have defined three operations of pranayama; inhalation, exhalation and suspension of the breath for a certain fixed number of moments. These operations are all controlled by the conscious will; they are parts of a deliberate exercise. But this fourth operation is involuntry and natural. When a man has gained complete control of the prana through exercises, or when he has reached a certain stage of spiritual development through devotion to God without practising pranayama, then his breathing may cease of its own accord at any time while he is deeply absorbed in concentration. This natural stoppage of the breath may continue for many seconds or minutes; he will not even be aware of it. In the state of samadhi, the breathing ceases altogether for hours at a time. This kind of suspension of the breath is not dangerous, because it can only take place when a man has sufficiently developed and is able to support it.

ततः क्षीयते प्रकाशावरणम् ॥ ५२ ॥

52. As the result of this, the covering of the Inner Light is removed.

"The Inner Light" is the light of spiritual discrimination between the Real and the unreal. "The covering" is made up of the ignorance produced by our past karmas. As the mind becomes purified through the practice of pranayama, this ignorance is gradually dispelled.

धारणासु च योग्यता मनसः ॥ ५३ ॥

53. The mind gains the power of concentration (dharana).

Patanjali will define concentration in the first aphorism of the next chapter.

स्वविषयासम्प्रयोगे चित्तस्वरूपानुकार
इवेन्द्रियाणां प्रत्याहारः ॥ ५४ ॥

54. When the mind is withdrawn from sense-objects, the sense-organs also withdraw themselves from their respective objects and thus are said to imitate the mind. This is known as pratyahara.

ततः परमा वश्यतेन्द्रियाणाम् ॥ ५५ ॥

55. Thence arises complete mastery over the senses.

Just as the provinces of a country are controlled by first taking over the central government, so we must begin by controlling the mind before we can control the rest of the body. As long as there is desire in the mind, the sense-organs will move eagerly and almost involuntarily toward the objects of desire. A man is aptly said to have a "roving eye" when his eyes, of their own accord, follow the figure of an attractive girl passing him in the street. The sense-organs are like animals which instinctively imitate their master. If the master is weak and subject to certain passions, then the sense-organs will imitate and even exaggerate his weakness, dragging him along after them as a child is dragged by a strong, untruly dog. But when the mind is strong and self-controlled the sense-organs become its orderly and obedient servants. They imitate its strength instead of its weakness. Every movement of the body expresses the self-control of the mind.

In order to control the mind, we have to get to know it. Few of us know, objectively, what the insides of our minds are really like. Our dominating fears and desires have become so familiar to us that we do not even notice them; they are like recurring drumbeats going on in the background of our thoughts. And so, as a preliminary exercise, it is good to spend some time every day simply watching our minds, listening to those drumbeats. We probably shall not like what we see and hear, but we must be very patient and objective. The mind, finding itself watched in this way, will gradually grow calmer. It becomes embarrassed, as it were, by its own greed and silliness. For no amount of outside criticism is so effective and so penetrating as our own simple self-inspection. If we continue this exercise regularly for several months, we shall certainly make some advance toward mental control.

III. POWERS

देशबन्धश्चित्तस्य धारणा ॥ १ ॥

1. Concentration (dharana) is holding the mind within a center of spiritual consciousness in the body, or fixing it on some divine form, either within the body or outside it.

The first five "limbs" of yoga have been discussed in the preceding chapter. Three remain: concentration (*dharana*), meditation (*dhyana*) and absorption (*samadhi*).

The centers of spiritual consciousness here referred to are the seven lotuses (II. 49-50). In order to concentrate, you must first fix your mind upon the Inner Light within one of these lotuses, as your teacher directs. Or you may concentrate upon the form of your Chosen Ideal, trying to visualize that form either within a lotus or outside your own body altogether.

तत्र प्रत्ययैकतानता ध्यानम् ॥ २ ॥

2. Meditation (dhyana) is an unbroken flow of thought toward the object of concentration.

In other words, meditation is prolonged concentration. The process of meditation is often compared to the pouring of oil from one vessel to another, in a steady, unbroken stream. We have seen (I.2) that Patanjali defines thought as a wave (vritti) in the mind. Ordinarily a thought-wave arises, remains in the mind for a moment, and then subsides, to be succeeded by another wave. In the practice of meditation, a succession of identical waves are raised in the mind; and this is done so quickly that no one wave is allowed to subside before another rises to take its place. The effect is therefore one of perfect continuity. If you shoot a hundred feet of film without moving your camera or your object, and then project the result on a screen, your audience might just as well be looking at a single still photograph. The many identical images are fused into one.

It will be seen from this definition that Patanjali's dhyana does not exactly correspond to our usual understanding of the word "meditation." By "meditation" we commonly mean a more or less discursive operation of the mind around a central idea. If, for example, we say that we have been meditating on Christ, we are apt to mean that we have not only tried to fix our minds on Christ's ideal form but have also been thinking about his teachings, his miracles, his disciples, his crucifixation, and so on. All this is very good, but it is a mere preliminary to what may properly be called dharana and dhyana.

तदेवार्थमात्रनिर्भासं स्वरूपशून्यमिव समाधिः ॥ ३ ॥

3. When, in meditation, the true nature of the object shines forth, not distorted by the mind of the perceiver, that is absorption (samadhi).

Ordinary sense-perception is distorted and coloured by the imagination of the perceiver. We decide in advance what it is we think we are going to see, and this preconception interferes with our vision. Great painters have often been violently attacked because they painted scenery as it actually looked, not as people thought it *ought* to look.

It is only in the supersensuous perception of samadhi that we see an object in the truth of its own nature, absolutely free from the distortions of our imagination.

Samadhi is, in fact, much more than perception; it is direct knowledge. When Sri Ramakrishna told Vivekananda, "I see God more real than I see you," he was speaking the literal truth. For Ramakrishna meant that he saw God in samadhi, while he saw Vivekananda with the eyes of his ordinary sense-perception which must necessarily retain a measure of distortion.

त्रयमेकत्र संयमः ॥ ४ ॥

4. When these three—concentration, meditation and absorption—are brought to bear upon one subject, they are called samyama.

Samyama is simply a convenient technical term which describes the three-fold process by which the true nature of an object is known.

तज्जयात् प्रज्ञाऽऽलोकः ॥ ५ ॥

5. Through mastery of samyama comes the light of knowledge.

तस्य भूमिषु विनियोगः ॥ ६ ॥

6. It must be applied stage by stage.

Patanjali warns us not to go too fast. It is no use attempting meditation before we have mastered concentration. It is no use trying to concentrate upon subtle objects until we are able to concentrate upon gross ones. Any attempt to take short cuts to knowledge of this kind is exceedingly dangerous. One may, for example, obtain certain psychic experiences while under the influence of drugs. But such experiences, so obtained, can bring no lasting spiritual benefits. On the contrary, they are generally followed by a relapse into complete agnosticism and despair.

The Vishnu Purana, one of the Hindu scriptures, teaches the practice of meditation by stages, beginning with the worship of God with form and culminating in the realization of the oneness of Atman and Brahman:

> Meditate on Vishnu, the Dweller in the heart of all beings, seated on a lotus within the rays of the sun, his body luminous, adorned with diadem, necklace, earrings, and bracelets of great luster, and holding conch shell and mace in his hands.
>
> Then the wise man should meditate upon the luminous, benign form of the Lord, without the conch shell and mace, but adorned with ornaments.
>
> As the mind becomes concentrated on the form, he must then keep his mind on the form without ornaments.
>
> Then he must meditate upon his oneness with the luminous form of the Lord.
>
> Lastly, he must let the form vanish and meditate upon the Atman.

त्रयमन्तरङ्गं पूर्वेभ्यः ॥ ७ ॥

7. These three are more direct aids to experience than the five limbs previously described.

That is to say, the first five limbs of yoga are only a form of training for the aspirant, to prepare him for the practice of samyama (concentration- meditation- absorption). The mind and senses have to be purified by the cultivation of ethical virtues and the whole organism has to be strengthened in order that it may be able to undergo the tremendous experiences that await it. But this is just the beginning. Even the perfection of samyama is just the beginning. For, whenever we are inclined to feel proud of some tiny indication of spiritual growth in ourselves, we shall do well to remember Brahmananda's amazing and sobering words: "Spiritual life begins *after* samadhi."

तदपि बहिरङ्गं निर्बीजस्य ॥ ८ ॥

8. But even these are not direct aids to the seedless samadhi.

The practice of samyama leads to the lower samadhi. But the "seedless" samadhi (nirvikalpa) demands a further and even more intense spiritual effort. (See chapter I, aphorism 51. Nearly everything Patanjali says here on the subject is simply recapitulation.) Patanjali now speaks of nirvikalpa:

व्युत्थान-निरोधसंस्कारयोरभिभव-प्रादुर्भावौ निरोधक्षणचित्तान्वयो निरोध-परिणामः ॥ ९ ॥

9. When the vision of the lower samadhi is suppressed by an act of conscious control, so that there are no longer any thoughts or visions in the mind, that is the achievement of control of the thought-waves of the mind.

तस्य प्रशान्तवाहिता संस्कारात् ॥ १० ॥

10. When this suppression of thought-waves becomes continuous, the mind's flow is calm.

सर्वार्थतैकाग्रतयोः क्षयोदयौ चित्तस्य समाधि-परिणामः ॥ ११ ॥

11. When all mental distractions disappear and the mind becomes one-pointed, it enters the state called samadhi.

शान्तोदितौ तुल्यप्रत्ययौ चित्तस्यैकाग्रता-
परिणामः ॥ १२ ॥

12. The mind becomes one-pointed when similar thought-waves arise in succession without any gaps between them.

It has been said that if the mind can be made to flow uninterruptedly toward the same object for twelve seconds, this may be called concentration. If the mind can continue in that concentration for twelve times twelve seconds (i.e., two minutes and twenty-four seconds), this may be called meditation. If the mind can continue in that meditation for twelve times two minutes and twenty-four seconds (i.e., twenty-eight minutes and forty-eight seconds), this will be the lower samadhi. And if the lower samadhi can be maintained for twelve times that period (i.e., five hours, forty-five minutes, and thirty-six seconds), this will lead to nirvikalpa samadhi.

एतेन भूतेन्द्रियेषु धर्मलक्षणावस्थापरिणामा
व्याख्याताः ॥ १३ ॥

13. In this state, it passes beyond the three kinds of changes which take place in subtle or gross matter, and in the organs: change of form, change of time and change of condition.

Vivekananda takes, as an example, a lump of gold. Change of form occurs when the gold is made first into a bracelet and theh into an earring. Change of time occurs as it gets older. Change of condition occurs when the bright gold becomes dull, or wears thin. Similar changes occur is subtle matter and in the thought-waves of the mind. The thought-waves may be of different kinds, may refer to different periods of time, and may vary in intensity. But the mind, in the state of samadhi, is beyond all three kinds of changes.

शान्तोदिताव्यपदेश्यधर्मानुपातो धर्मी ॥ १४ ॥

14. A compound object has attributes and is subject to change, either past, present or yet to be manifested.

क्रमान्यत्वं परिणामान्यत्वे हेतुः ॥ १५ ॥

15. The succession of these changes is the cause of manifold evolution.

Every object within the realm of differentiated matter has attributes and is a compound object, since it is made of the three gunas in varying combinations. As has already been explained in chapter I, the attributes of an object vary and change according to the action of the gunas and the constitution of the samskaras. Any object can change into any other object. Therefore, the enlightened yogi sees no essential difference between a piece of gold and a lump of mud. Hence, he acquires complete dispassion toward the objects of the phenomenal world.

परिणामत्रयसंयमादतीतानागतज्ञानम् ॥ १६ ॥

16. By making samyama on the three kinds of changes, one obtains knowledge of past and the future.

Patanjali now begins to describe the various occult powers and the methods by which they are acquired. All authorities, including Patanjali himself, regard occult powers as the greatest stumbling blocks in the path to truth. "Heaps of rubbish," Sri Ramakrishna calls them. Buddha told his disciples very definitely never to put their faith in miracles but to see truth in the eternal principles. Christ spoke sharply against those who "seek for a sign," and it is unfortunate that his strictures were not taken more seriously to heart by his followers.

Occult powers do, however, exist, and Patanjali, in his comprehensive treatise on yoga psychology, obviously cannot ignore them. We translate the aphorisms which follow for the sake of completeness, but we do so with a minimum of technical explanation. The sincere spiritual aspirant can have very little concern with such matters.

In the West, these powers are seldom exhibited, and are therefore the object of a good deal of skepticism. Yet they are all within each one of us and could be developed through constant practice. Western man has made a different choice. He has preferred to concentrate on the production of mechanical rather than psychological powers; and so, instead of telepathy we have the telephone, instead of levitation we have the helicopter, and instead of clairvoyance we have television. We may regret the materialism that is expressed by such a choice; but perhaps it is the lesser of two evils. A community of degenerated yogis, using psychic powers for business and political ends, would be even more unpleasant to live in than our own atom-wielding world. So let us stop hankering after the psychic powers and turn back to the true path toward spiritual growth, remembering Patanjali's warning. "They are powers in the worldly state, but they are obstacles to samadhi."

शब्दार्थप्रत्ययानामितरेतराध्यासात्सङ्करस्तत्-
प्रविभागसंयमात् सर्वभूतरुतज्ञानम् ॥ १७ ॥

17. By making samyama on the sound of a word, one's perception of its meaning, and one's reaction to it—three things which are ordinarily confused—one obtains understanding of all sounds uttered by living beings.

Ordinarily, we are aware of no distinction between hearing the sound of a word, understanding what it means, and reacting, in one way or another, to the information it contains. If someone shouts "fire" we jump to our feet in an instant. But the yogi is able to separate these three functions. By making this samyama, he can understand foreign languages and the sounds made by all kinds of animals.

संस्कारसाक्षात्करणात् पूर्वजातिज्ञानम् ॥ १८ ॥

18. By making samyama on previous thought-waves, one obtains knowledge of one's past lives.

When a thought-wave subsides, it remains within the mind, in a minute, subtle form. Therefore it can be revived as memory. And this memory can be made to extend backward into previous incarnations.

प्रत्ययस्य परचित्तज्ञानम् ॥ १९ ॥

19. By making samyama on the distinguishing marks of another man's body, one obtains knowledge of the nature of his mind.

न च तत् सालम्बनं तस्याविषयीभूतत्वात् ॥ २० ॥

20. But not of its contents, because that is not the object of the samyama.

In order to know the contents of another man's mind, the yogi would have to make a second samyama on the heart (aphorism 35 of this chapter).

कायरूपसंयमात्तद्ग्राह्यशक्ति-स्तम्भे
चक्षुःप्रकाशासंयोगेऽन्तर्धानम् ॥ २१ ॥

21. If one makes samyama on the form of one's body, obstructing its perceptibility and separating its power of manifestation from the eyes of the beholder, then one's body becomes invisible.

एतेन शब्दाद्यन्तर्धानमुक्तम् ॥ २२ ॥

22. Thus, also, its sounds cease to be heard.

In other words, it is possible for the yogi, while remaining present in a room, to obstruct the outward manifestation of his body in such a way that the senses of other people will be unable to detect it. The reality behind the outward manifestation will remain, but, since this reality cannot be detected by the gross sense-organs of others, the yogi will become unseen, unheard, unfelt, and so on.

सोपक्रमं निरुपक्रमं च कर्म तत्संयमादपरान्त-
ज्ञानमरिष्टेभ्यो वा ॥ २३ ॥

23. By making samyama on two kinds of karma—that which will soon bear fruit and that which will not bear fruit until later—or by recognizing the portents of death, a yogi may know the exact time of his separation from the body.

Portents of death include various physical and psychical phenomena, together with visions of supernatural beings. (It is better not to be too explicit here, lest the reader should alarm himself unduly!). Hindus believe that it is very important to know the exact hour of one's death in advance, because the thoughts one is thinking at that moment will to some degree determine the nature of one's afterlife.

मैत्र्यादिषु बलानि ॥ २४ ॥

24. By making samyama on friendliness, compassion, etc., one develops the powers of these qualities.

The reference here is to aphorism 33 of chapter I: "friendliness toward the happy, compassion for the unhappy, delight in the virtuous." The yogi who masters this samyama has the power of giving joy to everyone he meets, and relieving him from pain and care.

बलेषु हस्तिबलादीनि ॥ २५ ॥

25. By making samyama on any kind of strength, such as that of the elephant, one obtains that strength.

प्रवृत्त्यालोकन्यासात् सूक्ष्म-व्यवहित-
विप्रकृष्टज्ञानम् ॥ २६ ॥

26. By making samyama on the Inner Light one obtains knowledge of what is subtle, hidden, or far distant.

The Inner Light is the light of the lotus within the heart, referred to in aphorism 36 of chapter I.

भुवनज्ञानं सूर्ये संयमात् ॥ २७ ॥

27. By making samyama on the sun, one gains knowledge of the cosmic spaces.

चन्द्रे ताराव्यूहज्ञानम् ॥ २८ ॥

28. By making samyama on the moon, one gains knowledge of the arrangement of the stars.

ध्रुवे तद्गतिज्ञानम् ॥ २९ ॥

29. By making samyama on the polestar, one gains knowledge of the motions of the stars.

It has already been remarked that there is a strong resemblance between the cosmology of Patanjali and the theories of modern atomic physics. Yet the ancient Hindus had, as far as we know, practically no scientific apparatus of any accuracy. This fact alone would seem to offer some proof of the validity of the psychic powers. For how else could these sages have formed such a correct and comprehensive picture of the nature of the universe? This knowledge cannot have been based, as ours is, simply upon sense-perception assisted by instruments.

नाभिचक्रे कायव्यूहज्ञानम् ॥ ३० ॥

30. By making samyama on the navel, one gains knowledge of the constitution of the body.

कण्ठकूपे क्षुत्पिपासानिवृत्तिः ॥ ३१ ॥

31. By making samyama on the hollow of the throat, one stills hunger and thirst.

कूर्मनाड्यां स्थैर्यम् ॥ ३२ ॥

32. By making samyama on the tube within the chest, one acquires absolute motionlessness.

The motionlessness, for example, of the snake or the lizard. This enables the yogi to meditate undisturbed by the involuntary movements of his body.

मूर्धज्योतिषि सिद्धदर्शनम् ॥ ३३ ॥

33. By making samyama on the radiance within the back of the head, one becomes able to see the celestial beings.

The radiance within the back of the head is not to be confused with the radiance of the seventh lotus, the highest center of spiritual consciousness, which is situated at the head (see II, 50).

प्रातिभाद्वा सर्वम् ॥ ३४ ॥

34. All these powers of knowledge may also come to one whose mind is spontaneously enlightened through purity.

When the mind has reached a very high state of purification, the psychic powers may come to it spontaneously and unbidden, without the making of any samyama.

हृदये चित्त-संवित् ॥ ३५ ॥

35. By making samyama on the heart, one gains knowledge of the contents of the mind.

सत्त्वपुरुषयोरत्यन्तासंकीर्णयोः प्रत्ययाविशेषाद्
भोगः परार्थत्वात् स्वार्थसंयमात् पुरुषज्ञानम् ॥ ३६ ॥

36. The power of enjoyment arises from a failure to discriminate between the Atman and the sattwa guna, which are totally different. The sattwa guna

is merely the agent of the Atman, which is independent, existing only for its own sake. By making samyama on the independence of the Atman, one gains knowledge of the Atman.

In the ordinary state of consciousness, the highest enjoyment we can know is the joy inspired by the guna of sattwa. This seems to us, in our ignorance, to be identical with the joy of the pure Atman; but it is not. Sattwa, even in its purest state, is still a guna; and sattwic joy still contains a measure of egotism. What we have to understand is that the gunas are only agents of the Atman, and that sattwic joy is only a pale reflection of the joy of the Atman, which is without egotism and entirely independent of the gunas. By making this samyama and discriminating between Atman and sattwa, the yogi passes beyond earthly enjoyment into the joy of the Atman itself.

ततः प्रतिभश्रावणवेदनादर्शास्वादवार्ता
जायन्ते ॥ ३७ ॥

37. Hence one gains the knowledge due to spontaneous enlightenment, and obtains supernatural powers of hearing, touch, sight, taste and smell.

ते समाधावुपसर्गा व्युत्थाने सिद्धयः ॥ ३८ ॥

38. They are powers in the wordly state, but they are obstacles to samadhi.

बन्धकारणशैथिल्यात् प्रचारसंवेदनाच्च चित्तस्य
परशरीरावेशः ॥ ३९ ॥

39. When the bonds of the mind caused by karma have been loosened, the yogi can enter into the body of another by knowledge of the operation of its nerve-currents.

"The yogi, says Vivekananda, "can enter a dead body and make it get up and move, even while he himself is working in another body. Or he can enter a living body, and hold that man's mind and organs in check, and for the time being act through the body of that man."

This recalls a story that is told about Shankara, the great philosopher and saint. When Shankara was still a boy in his teens, there was a philosopher named Mandan Misra who held that the life of the householder was far superior to that of the monk; an opinion which was widely shared throughout India. Shankara determined to hold a debate with Misra, knowing that if he could convert him he could also convert Misra's many disciples. After considerable difficulties, he succeeded in making Misra agree to this. It was understood that Shankara, if he lost, should become a householder, and that Misra, if he lost, should become a monk. At Shankara's suggestion, Misra's wife Bharati, herself a famous scholar, acted as umpire.

After a debate of several days, Misra was ready to admit total defeat. But Bharati said to Shankara: "Wait. Husband and wife are one person. You have only defeated half of us. Now you must debate with me. You may know all about philosophy, but I choose another subject. I choose sex. It is a great science. Before you can claim either of us as your disciples, you will have to debate with me and defeat me on that."

For the moment Shankara was baffled. As a monk and a mere boy, he knew nothing whatever about sex. However, a plan occured to him. He asked for a month's delay; and this Bharati granted.

At this time, it so happened that a king named Amaraka lay dying. Shankara told his disciples to hide his own body in a safe place and take great care of it. Then, by yoga power, he left his body and entered the newly dead body of the king. Amaraka apparently revived, and continued to rule the kingdom under the guidance of Shankara.

Shankara-Amaraka proved to be a brilliant and just ruler, winning the admiration of all. But Amaraka's two wives soon realized that something extraordinary had happened. For the new Amaraka not only showed astonishingly youthful energy; he seemed as ignorant of sexual love as a baby. Meanwhile, the preoccupations of kingship and domestic life began to cloud Shankara's mind. He began to forget what he had done, why he had done it, and who he was. He began to believe that he really was Amaraka, and not Shankara.

Shankara's disciples learned of this. Since monks were not admitted to the court, they disguised themselves as wandering musicians and so came into his presence. Then they began to sing the poem called "Moha Mudgaram," "The Shattering of Delusion," which Shankara himself had composed:

Beloved, strange are the World's ways and vast thy ignorance.
Who is thy wife, and who thy son? Whose art thou?
From what place come hence?
Ponder this in thy heart and bow to God in reverence.

The words recalled Shankara to awareness of his own identity. The body of King Amaraka fell dead to the ground as Shankara left it and returned to his own body.

Later, when Shankara appeared at Misra's house, Bharati knew at once what it was that he had done, for she also possessed yoga powers, and she admitted defeat without further debate.

उदानजयाज्जलपङ्कण्टकादिष्वसङ्ग
उत्क्रान्तिश्च ॥ ४० ॥

40. By controlling the nerve-currents that govern the lungs and the upper part of the body, the yogi can walk on water and swamps, or on thorns and similar objects, and he can die at will.

समानजयात् प्रज्वलनम् ॥ ४१ ॥

41. By controlling the force which governs the prana, he can surround himself with a blaze of light.

This is the force which regulates the various functions of the vital energy (prana). One of the brother-disciples of Sri Ramakrishna actually had this power; and it is recorded that he once used it to light the path for Ramakrishna on a dark night. However, Ramakrishna later found it necessary to take the power away from him because it was making him dangerously egotistic.

श्रोत्राकाशयोः सम्बन्धसंयमाद्दिव्यं श्रोत्रम् ॥ ४२ ॥

42. By making samyama on the relation between the ear and the ether, one obtains supernatural powers of hearing.

कायाकाशयोः सम्बन्धसयमाल्लघुतूलसमापत्तेश्चा-
काशगमनम् ॥ ४३ ॥

43. By making samyama on the relation between the body and the ether, or by acquiring through

meditation the lightness of cotton fibre, the yogi can fly through the air.

बहिरकल्पिता वृत्तिर्महाविदेहा ततः
प्रकाशावरणक्षयः ॥ ४४ ॥

44. By making samyama on the thought-waves of the mind when it is separated from the body—the state known as the Great Disincarnation—all coverings can be removed from the light of knowledge.

Like aphorism 39, this refers to the yoga power of withdrawing the mind from one's own body in order to make it pass into the body of another. In this state of withdrawal, the "Great Disincarnation," the mental coverings composed of rajas and tamas dwindle away and the light of sattwa is revealed.

स्थूल-स्वरूप-सूक्ष्मान्वयार्थवत्त्वसंयमा-
द्भूतजयः ॥ ४५ ॥

45. By making samyama on the gross and subtle forms of the elements, on their essential characteristics and the inherence of the gunas in them, and on the experiences they provide for the individual, one gains mastery of the elements.

ततोऽणिमादिप्रादुर्भावः कायसम्पत्तद्धर्मानभि-
घातश्च ॥ ४६ ॥

46. Hence one gains the power of becoming as tiny as an atom and all similar powers: also perfection of the body, which is no longer subject to the obstruction of the elements.

Not only can the yogi become as tiny as an atom but as huge as a mountain, as heavy as lead, or as light as air. And the elements cease to obstruct him. He can pass through rock. He can hold his hand in the fire, unburned. He can walk through water, unwetted. He can stand firm against a hurricane.

रूप-लावण्य-बल-वज्रसहननत्वानि
कायसम्पत् ॥ ४७ ॥

47. Perfection of the body includes beauty, grace, strength and the hardness of a thunderbolt.

ग्रहण-स्वरूपास्मितान्वयार्थवत्वसंयमादिन्द्रिय-
जयः ॥ ४८

48. By making samyama on the transformation that the sense-organs undergo when they contact objects, on the power of illumination of the sense-organs, on the ego-sense, on the gunas which constitute the organs, and on the experiences they provide for the individual, one gains mastery of the organs.

ततो मनोजवित्वं विकरणभावः प्रधानजयश्च ॥ ४९ ॥

49. Hence the body gains the power of movement as rapid as that of the mind, the power of using the sense-organs outside the confines of the body, and the mastery of Prakriti.

Aphorism 48 describes a progressive samyama on all the separate phases of an act of cognition.

The power of using the sense-organs outside the confines of the body, mentioned in aphorism 49, enables one to exercise clairvoyance and clairaudience. Mastery of Prakriti, the primal cause, gives the yogi control of all the effects evolved from Prakriti — in other words, control of Nature.

सत्त्वपुरुषान्यताख्यातिमात्रस्य सर्वभावाधिष्ठातृत्वं सर्वज्ञातृत्वञ्च ॥ ५० ॥

50. By making samyama on the discrimination between the sattwa guna and the Atman, one gains omnipotence and omniscience.

This discrimination has already been discussed (aphorism 36 of this chapter).

तद्वैराग्यादपि दोषबीजक्षये कैवल्यम् ॥ ५१ ॥

51. By giving up even these powers, the seed of evil is destroyed and liberation follows.

The "seed of evil" is ignorance. Because of ignorance, man forgets that he is the Atman and creates for himself the illusion of a private, separate ego-personality. This ego-personality is intent upon satisfying its desires, and acquiring possessions and powers over external nature. Of all powers, the psychic powers are, from the standpoint of the ego, the most desirable; and, of the psychic powers, omnipotence and omniscience (to which Patanjali has referred in the previous aphorism) are obviously the greatest. The yogi who has held even these powers within his grasp and nevertheless renounced them, has rejected the ultimate temptation of the ego. Henceforth, he is freed from bondage. (For example, Christ rejected the psychic powers offered to him by Satan in the wilderness.)

स्थान्युपनिमन्त्रणे सङ्गस्मयाकरणं
पुनरनिष्ट-प्रसङ्गात् ॥ ५२ ॥

52. When tempted by the invisible beings in high places, let the yogi feel neither allured nor flattered; for he is in danger of being caught once more by ignorance.

"The invisible beings in high places" are the fallen yogis already referred to (I, 19) who have reached the state of disincarnate gods or become merged in the forces of Nature. Such beings have failed to find liberation precisely because they yielded to the temptations of the psychic powers. Therefore, it is said, they are jealous of those who seem about to overcome these temptations, and they try to drag them back into ignorance. In the commentary on Patanjali's aphorisms which is attributed to Vyasa, the allurements offered to the yogi by "those in high places" are described, quaintly but forcefully, as follows: "Sir, will you seat yourself here? Will you rest here? You might enjoy this pleasure. You might find this maiden attractive. This elixir will banish old age and death. In this chariot you can fly through the air. Over there are trees which grant all wishes. That heavenly stream will give you happiness. Those sages know everything. These nymphs are peerlessly beautiful, and you will not find them cold. Your eyes and ears will become supernaturally keen, your body will shine like a diamond. In consequence of your distinguished virtues, honoured Sir, you are entitled to all these rewards. Please enter into this heaven which is unfailing, ageless, deathless, and dear to the gods."

Thus tempted, the yogi is advised to reply as follows: "I have been baked on the dreadful coals of reincarnation. I have writhed in the darkness of rebirth and death. Now at last I have found the lamp of yoga which dispels the shadows of ignorance. How then can I, who have seen its light, be led astray once more by sensual things?"

The great Hindu teachers all believed that a yogi's spiritual development might be interfered with by external forces — by the disincarnate gods, by beings on the psychic or subtle plane of matter, or by earthbound spirits. And this belief is symbolized in the traditional Hindu ritualistic worship, which begins as follows:

First, the worshipper must try to feel the presence of God everywhere, as the all-pervading Existence. Then he must feel that the doors of his senses are locked and that he has entered into the shrine of his own heart, where God dwells. He must say: "As a man with eyes wide open sees the sky before him, so the seers see always the supreme truth of God." Trying to imagine that he has already gained this power of spiritual sight, he now opens his eyes, repeating his mantram as he does so. He must look about him, trying to see the presence of God in everything he sees and to know that by the power of the mantram the obstacles created by the disincarnate gods are being removed.

Next he must throw a spoonful of water straight up into the air, as if into the psychic realm, invoking the protective power of God to remove all psychic obstacles.

Finally, he must take some rice between his right thumb and forefinger, and scatter it in a circle, saying: "May the earth-bound spirits and the spirits that create obstacles be dissolved by the will of the Lord Shiva." The earthbound spirits are said to be the spirits of those who have committed suicide. They are earthbound because they still have to work out the karma which they have tried to reject by their act. The worshipper is praying that they may be released from their present form and thus set free to develop toward liberation. Sometimes, a food offering is given to the earthbound spirits to propitiate them, and they are told either to leave the place or to remain and watch the worship without interfering, from a respectful distance.

It is only after performing these preliminary ceremonies that the worshipper can proceed to the direct ritualistic worship of his Chosen Deity.

Up to a certain point, temptation increases with spiritual growth. As the aspirant ceases to be a mere beginner and gains some mystical experience, his personality becomes magnetic. He finds that he can exert psychological power over others, and also sexual attraction. At the same time, his own senses grow keener and more capable of enjoyment. It is therefore easy for him to become involved in power and sex-relationships which will make him forget his original purpose. The very people who are drawn to him because of the god-like quality they see in his nature may be the ones who are most responsible for his gradual alienation from God. But, as Sri Krishna tells us; "no one who seeks Brahman ever comes to an evil end." And so, even when such a lapse takes place, we may believe that the spiritual aspirant will eventually find his way back to the path, and that those who tempted him from it will also, to some extent, have gained spiritual benefit from their association with him.

क्षण-तत्क्रमयोः संयमाद्विवेकजं ज्ञानम् ॥ ५३ ॥

53. By making samyama on single moments and on their sequence in time, one gains discriminative knowledge.

By a "moment" is meant an indivisible unit, the smallest imaginable instant. A moment is regarded by Patanjali as an object. It belongs to the order of external phenomena, like a dog, a diamond, or a tree. But a sequence of moments

— that is to say, what we call "time" — is not an object; it is only a structure created by our minds, an idea.

By making samyama on single moments and on their sequence in time, the yogi comes to realize that the entire universe passes through a change within every single moment. Hence, he understands that the nature of the universe is transitory. This understanding is what is meant by discriminative knowledge. Because the yogi's mind is not subject to the illusion of "time," he can understand the real nature of his experiences. The rest of us, who think in terms of time-sequences, are constantly generalizing our sensations, mentally carrying over the sensation of one moment into the next and the next. We say, "I was sad the whole afternoon," when, in fact, we were only sad at 2:15, 2:37, 3:01, and so forth. Thus we not only deceive ourselves but suffer much imaginary pain. There is a Zen Buddhist technique for enduring torture by breaking up the time-sequence, and concentrating only upon what is happening in each moment of the immediate present. In this way, suffering can be robbed of its continuity and made much more tolerable. For suffering is largely composed of our memory of past pain and our fear of repeated pain in the future, and this memory and this fear are dependent on our consciousness of a time-sequence.

जाति-लक्षण-देशैरन्यताऽनवच्छेदात्तुल्ययोस्ततः
प्रतिपत्तिः ॥ ५४ ॥

54. Thus one is able to distinguish between two exactly similar objects, which cannot be distinguished by their species, characteristic marks, or positions in space.

Suppose you took two exactly similar, newly minted coins, showed first one, then the other; then changed them behind your back and showed them again. The yogi who had made this samyama would, according to Patanjali, be able to tell you correctly which one you had showed him first.

The spiritual value of this power of discrimination lies, of course, in one's ability to distinguish always between the Atman and the non-Atman, the outward appearance, however deceptive the latter may be.

तारकं सर्वविषयं सर्वथाविषयमक्रमञ्चेति
विवेकजं ज्ञानम् ॥ ५५ ॥

55. This discriminative knowledge delivers a man from the bondage of ignorance. It comprehends all objects simultaneously, at every moment of their existence and in all their modifications.

Ordinary knowledge based on sense-perception is sequence. We learn one fact about a given object, then another fact, then more and more facts. But the yogi who possesses discriminative knowledge understands objects totally and immediately. If, for example, he meets another human being, he knows him at once in all his past and future modifications, as a baby, a youth, an adult, and an old man. Such knowledge is infinite; it is within eternity, not time. It delivers a man from the bondage of karma and ignorance.

सत्त्वपुरुषयोः शुद्धिसाम्ये कैवल्यमिति ॥ ५६ ॥

56. Perfection is attained when the mind becomes as pure as the Atman itself.

When all the thought-waves in the mind have been stilled, the mind holds nothing but pure, undifferentiated consciousness. In this state, it is one with the Atman. Sri Ramakrishna used to say: "The pure mind and the Atman are the same."

IV. LIBERATION

जन्मौषधि-मन्त्र-तपः-समाधिजाः सिद्धयः ॥ १ ॥

1. The psychic powers may be obtained either by birth, or by means of drugs, or by the power of words, or by the practice of austerities, or by concentration.

Some are born with psychic powers as the result of their struggles in previous lives. And not psychic powers merely, but real spiritual genius. Such are those most mysterious of all human beings, the "natural" saints, who are filled with the knowledge and love of God even in early childhood and grow up seemingly untouched by the temptations of worldliness.

In the Bhagavad-Gita, Arjuna asks: "Suppose a man has faith, but does not struggle hard enough? His mind wanders away from the practice of yoga and he fails to reach perfection. What will become of him then?" And Sri Krishna answers: "Even if a man falls away from the practice of yoga, he will still win the heaven of the doers of good deeds, and dwell there many long years. After that, he will be reborn into the home of pure and prosperous parents.... He will then regain that spiritual discernment which he acquired in his former body; and so he will strive harder than ever for perfection. Because of his practices in the previous life, he will be driven on toward union with Brahman, even in spite of himself."

Certain drugs may produce visions but these are invariably psychic — not spiritual, as is commonly believed. Furthermore, they may cause prolonged spiritual dryness and disbelief and may even do permanent damage to the brain.

The repetition of sacred words or mantrams is, as we have been told, an invaluable aid to spiritual progress. There are also special mantrams which produce psychic powers.

The practice of austerities enormously strengthens the aspirant's will power. Hence also the psychic powers may be obtained.

But concentration is the surest of all the means of obtaining the psychic powers. This has been thoroughly discussed in the previous chapter.

जात्यन्तरपरिणामः प्रकृत्यापूरात् ॥ २ ॥

2. The transformation of one species into another is caused by the inflowing of nature.

निमित्तमप्रयोजकं प्रकृतीनां वरणभेदस्तु ततः
क्षेत्रिकवत् ॥ ३ ॥

3. Good or bad deeds are not the direct causes of the transformation. They only act as breakers of the obstacles to natural evolution; just as a farmer breaks down the obstacles in a water course, so that water flows through by its own nature.

Here, Patanjali explains the Hindu theory of evolution of species by means of an illustration from agriculture. The farmer who irrigates one of his fields from a reservoir does not have to fetch the water. The water is there already. All the farmer has to do is to open a sluice gate or break down a dam, and the water flows into the field by the natural force of gravity.

The "water" is the force of evolution which, according to Patanjali, each one of us carries within him, only waiting to be released from the "reservoir." By our acts we "open the sluice gate," the water runs down into the field; the field bears its crop and is thereby transformed. In other words, the form of the next rebirth is determined. "All progress and power are already in every man," says Vivekananda. "Perfection is in every man's nature, only it is barred in and prevented from taking its proper course. If anyone can take the bar off, in rushes nature."

To pursue the image of the reservoir, the performance of bad deeds and the consequent accumulation of bad karma is like breaking the dam at the wrong place and thereby causing a disastrous flood which will ruin and disfigure the field. If this happens, the water is not to blame; it is in its nature to cause change of one kind or another. It has to be properly directed. And for that the farmer is entirely responsible.

It will be seen that there is a radical difference between the ancient Hindu and the modern Western theories of evolution. As Vivekananda puts it: "The two causes of evolution advanced by the moderns, *viz.*, sexual selection and survival of the fittest, are inadequate. Suppose human knowledge to have advanced so much as to eliminate competition, both from the function of acquiring physical sustenance and the acquiring of a mate. Then, according to the moderns, human progress will stop and the race will die. But Patanjali declares that the true secret of evolution is the manifestation of the perfection which is already in every being that this perfection has been barred and the infinite tide behind is struggling to express itself Even when all competition has ceased this perfect nature behind will make us go forward until every one has become perfect. Therefore there is no reason to believe that competition is necessary to progress. In the animal the man was suppressed, but, as soon as the door was opened, out rushed man. So, in man there is the potential god, kept in by the locks and bars of ignorance. When knowledge breaks these bars, the god becomes manifest."

निर्माणचित्तान्यस्मितामात्रात् ॥ ४ ॥

4. The ego-sense alone can create minds.

प्रवृत्तिभेदे प्रयोजकं चित्तमेकमनेकेषाम् ॥ ५ ॥

5. Though the activities of the different created minds are various, the one original mind controls them all.

These two aphorisms refer to the psychic power of creating for oneself a number of subsidiary minds and bodies, over which the original mind maintains control. Since it is the ego-sense which creates an individual mind (I, 17), it is theoretically evident that this ego-sense should be able to create subsidiary minds, revolving like satellites around the original. The idea is that the yogi might wish to have several minds and bodies in order to exhaust all of his karma more quickly. But the wisdom of this plan would seem to be doubtful. There is a story of a king who made himself many bodies, hoping in this way to exhaust his craving for sexual enjoyment. But finally he abandoned the attempt declaring: "Lust is never satisfied by gratification; it only flares up more and more, like a fire fed with butter."

Patanjali seems to admit this in the next aphorism:

तत्र ध्यानजमनाशयम् ॥ ६ ॥

6. Of the various types of mind, only that which is purified by 'samadhi is freed from all latent impressions of karma and from all cravings.

In other words, karma can only be exhausted by spiritual realization; never be mere satiety of experience.

कर्माशुक्लाकृष्णं योगिनस्त्रिविधमितरेषाम् ॥ ७ ॥

7. The karma of the yogi is neither white nor black. The karma of others is of three kinds; white, black, or mixed.

The karma of ordinary people is either black (bad), white (good), or mixed. But when a man has attained samadhi his acts will cease to produce karmas for him, of any kind (see I, 11). Nevertheless, since the illumined yogi continues to act, karmas *are* being produced, and there may even be some admixture of evil in them. Who gets these karmas? Shankara gives an interesting answer to this question. He says that those who love the illumined yogi will receive the good effects of his karmas, while those who hate him will receive the bad.

Such is not the case, however, with an *avatar* or divine incarnation. An avatar, such as Krishna, Christ or Ramakrishna, is an actual incarnation of the Godhead. He enters the phenomenal world by an act of grace and divine free will, not because he is forced to do so by the karmas of previous births. He comes into the world without karmas, and his acts in this world produce none. Therefore, the effects of his karmas cannot be received by others, either for good or for ill.

In Hindu religious literature, there are numerous stories of men who hated God or an avatar. Kamsa tried to have the infant Krishna murdered, just as Herod tried to murder the baby Jesus. Shishupal fought with Krishna. Ravana fought with Rama. And, in all these instances, these men attained liberation. This may sound strange to a Christian; but the point made here is the spiritual value of intense feeling. It is best to love an avatar, but it is better to hate him passionately than to be indifferent to him. Indifference, as always, is the worst sin. Rajas is spiritually higher than tamas. By way of rajas, we may reach sattw[illegible] by way of hatred we may find love. The ancie[illegible]ore, have disagreed with Dante[illegible]not in the lowest circle [illegible]

तत[illegible]गुणानामेवाभिव्यक्ति-

वासनानाम् ॥ ८ ॥

8. **Of the tendencies produced by these three kinds of karma, only those are manifested for which the conditions are favourable.**

In any particular incarnation, a man's condition is determined by the balance of his karmas. Suppose that balance is very favourable, and he is born to become a monk and a spiritual teacher. He will still have some bad karmas which, under less favourable conditions, would produce bad tendencies. But, because he has to live up to his vocation and set a good example to his pupils, these tendencies will be kept in abeyance, and only his good tendencies will be manifested. So this aphorism stresses the great importance of right environment, association with those who are spiritually minded. If you are born as a dog, you may still have good tendencies, but they will be greatly restricted by your dog condition. You have to act in accordance with your animal nature.

जाति-देश-काल-व्यवहितानामप्यानन्तर्यं

स्मृतिसंस्कारयोरेकरूपत्वात् ॥ ९ ॥

9. Because of our memory of past tendencies, the chain of cause and effect is not broken by change of species, space or time.

By "memory," Patanjali does not mean conscious remembering, but unconscious co-ordination of the impressions received in past lives with the actions and thoughts of our present life. Karma — the chain of cause and effect — is absolutely continuous. If, in the course of many incarnations, we change our species — evolving from animal into man, or from man into some non-human type of being — our karma will still continue to operate. However, as noted in the preceding aphorism, only those tendencies appropriate to our species and condition will be manifested in any one life; the rest will be held in abeyance until we reincarnate into another species and conditions appropriate to them.

तासामनादित्वं चाशिषो नित्यत्वात् ॥ १० ॥

10. Since the desire to exist has always been present our tendencies cannot have had any beginning.

As we have already learned, Hindu philosophy regards creation and dissolution as a beginningless and endless process. Karma has always operated, always created tendencies. There was no primal act. It is only as individuals that we can set ourselves free from karma by unlearning this desire to exist on the phenomenal level and realizing the Atman, our eternal nature. Suppose every individual in the universe were to achieve liberation, would the universe cease to exist? Being still within time, none of us can answer such a question. In fact, the question cannot properly be asked. For the phenomenal universe is in perpetual transition from "was" to "will be"; while the Atman is eternally "now." And though the human, time-bounded mind can make this statement, it cannot possibly understand what it really means.

हेतुफलाश्रयालम्बनैः संगृहीतत्वादेषामभावे तदभावः ॥ ११ ॥

11. **Our subconscious tendencies depend upon cause and effect. They have their basis in the mind, and they are stimulated by the sense-objects. If all these are removed, the tendencies are destroyed.**

Karma can only operate and produce tendencies as long as certain causes are present. These causes (II, 3) are ignorance, egoism, attachment, aversion, and the desire to cling to life. The effects of these causes (II, 13) are rebirth, a long or a short life, and the experiences of pleasure and pain. Basically, karma is rooted in ignorance of the Atman. Remove this ignorance, and you destroy karma.

"This vast universe is a wheel," says the Swetaswatara Upanishad. "Upon it are all creatures that are subject to birth, death, and rebirth. Round and round it turns, and never stops. It is the wheel of Brahman. As long as the individual self thinks it is separate from Brahman, it revolves upon the wheel..... But when through the grace of Brahman it realizes its identity with him, it revolves upon the wheel no longer. It achieves immortality."

अतीतानागतं स्वरूपतोऽस्त्यध्व भेदाद्धर्माणाम् ॥ १२ ॥

12. **There is the form and expression we call "past," and the form and expression we call "future";**

both exist within the object, at all times. Form and expression vary according to time—past, present or future.

ते व्यक्त-सूक्ष्मा गुणात्मानः ॥ १३ ॥

13. They are either manifest or subtle, according to the nature of the gunas.

परिणामैकत्वाद्वस्तुतत्वम् ॥ १४ ॥

14. Since the gunas work together within every change of form and expression, there is a unity in all things.

The Gita teaches: "That which is non-existent can never come into being, and that which is can never cease to be." The forms and expressions of an object may change, but all these changes of form and expression have existed, and will continue to exist, potentially, within the object. The past and future exist within the object in an unmanifested, subtle form. Nevertheless, they are there. Nothing in the universe is lost.

All objects are compounded of the gunas. The gunas may project a gross manifestation; that is to say, a visible and tangible object. Or they may project a subtle manifestation, not apparent to the senses. Further, they may alter their interrelationship — so that, for example, rajas becomes dominant in place of sattwa; in which case, the form of the object may change entirely. But, since the three gunas never cease to be present in one or another combination, the object preserves an essential unity, even in the diversity of its forms and expressions.

Hence we see that the same mind exists essentially throughout the many rebirths of the individual. It is only the play of the gunas that makes the mind alter its form and expression in different incarnations; now seeming predominantly evil, now predominantly good. In the mind of a good man, the past evil impressions still exist in subtle form; and the future impressions, whatever they are to be, exist also.

How, then, is liberation possible? Patanjali has already answered this question several times; and he has restated his answer in aphorism 11 of this chapter. Our subconscious tendencies, he says, have their basis in the mind. Therefore a man must cease to identify himself with the mind, in order to win liberation. When he knows beyond doubt that he is the Atman, and not the mind, he is made free from his karma.

The mind of a liberated soul, with all its past, present and future impressions, has no longer any existence as a phenomenal object; but it is not lost. It is resolved back into undifferentiated matter, Prakriti. There is a Hindu saying that the knowledge of the illumined soul turns both present and future into past.

वस्तुसाम्ये चित्तभेदात्तयोर्विभक्तः पन्थाः ॥ १५ ॥

15. The same object is perceived in different ways by different minds. Therefore the mind must be other than the object.

न चैकचित्ततन्त्रं वस्तु तदप्रमाणकं तदा किं स्यात् ॥

15A. The object cannot be said to be dependent on the perception of a single mind. For, if this were the case, the object could be said to be non-existent when that single mind was not perceiving it.

In these two aphorisms, Patanjali refutes the philosophy of subjective idealism. Following Sankhya philosophy, he admits the reality of an objective world which is independent of our mental perception. Furthermore, he points out that the perceptions of one individual vary from those of another. The example given by the commentators is that of a young and beautiful married woman. She brings joy to her husband, causes other women to be jealous of her beauty, arouses lust in the lustful, and is regarded with indifference by the man of self-control. Which of these observers knows her as she really is? None of them. The object-in-itself cannot be known by sense-perception. (I, 43).

तदुपरागापेक्षित्वाच्चित्तस्य वस्तु ज्ञाताज्ञातम् ॥ १६ ॥

16. An object is known or unknown, depending upon the moods of the mind.

सदा ज्ञाताश्चित्तवृत्तयस्तत्प्रभोः पुरुषस्यापरि-
णामित्वात् ॥ १७ ॥

17. Because the Atman, the Lord of the mind, is unchangeable, the mind's fluctuations are always known to it.

न तत् स्वाभासं दृश्यत्वात् ॥ १८ ॥

18. The mind is not self-luminous, since it is an object of perception.

एकसमये चोभयानवधारणम् ॥ १९ ॥

19. And since it cannot perceive both subject and object simultaneously.

As we saw at the very beginning of this book (I, 2), the mind is not the seer, but the instrument of the Atman, which is eternally conscious. The mind is only intermittently conscious of objects, and its perceptions of them vary according to its own fluctuations. The mind is changing all the time, and so is the object of perception. The Atman alone, by remaining unchanged, provides a standard by which all perception can be measured. Vivekananda gives the example of a train in motion, with a carriage moving alongside of it. "It is possible to find the motion of both these to a certain extent. But still something else is necessary. Motion can only be perceived when there is something else which is not moving... You must complete the series by knowing something which never changes."

The mind is just as much an object of perception as any object it perceives in the external world. The mind is not self-luminous; that is to say, it is not a light-giver, like the sun; but a light-reflector, like the moon. The light-giver, the "sun," is the Atman, and the mind only shines and perceives by the reflected light of the Atman.

If the mind were self-luminous, it would be able to perceive both itself and an external object simultaneously. This it cannot do. While it is perceiving an external object, it cannot reflect on itself, and vice versa.

चित्तान्तरदृश्ये बुद्धिबुद्धेरतिप्रसङ्गः स्मृति-
सङ्करश्च ॥ २० ॥

20. If one postulates a second mind to perceive the first, then one would have to postulate an infinite number of minds; and this would cause confusion of memory.

If a philosopher — in order to avoid admitting the existence of the Atman — were to suggest that the mind is really two minds, a knower and an object of knowledge, then he would find himself in difficulty. For if mind A is known by mind B, then one must postulate a mind C as the knower of B, a mind D as the knower of C, and so forth. There would be an infinite regress, as in a room walled with mirrors. Furthermore, since each of these minds would have an individual memory, the function of remembering would be reduced to utter confusion.

चितेरप्रतिसंक्रमायास्तदाकारपत्तौ स्वबुद्धि-
संवेदनम् ॥ २१ ॥

21. The pure consciousness of the Atman is unchangeable. As the reflection of its consciousness falls upon the mind, the mind takes the form of the Atman and appears to be conscious.

द्रष्टृदृश्योपरक्तं चित्तं सर्वार्थम् ॥ २२ ॥

22. The mind is able to perceive because it reflects both the Atman and the objects of perception.

The mind stands midway, as it were, between Atman and external object. Its power to perceive the object is only borrowed from the Atman. In a perfectly dark room, a mirror cannot reflect the man who stands before it. But when a light is brought in, the mirror immediately "perceives" the man.

Similarly, the individual soul is known to Hindu philosophy as the "reflected", or the "shadow Atman". It has no separate existence. It is only the reflection of the

Atman upon the mind, which gives rise to a separate sense of ego.

तदसंख्येयवासनाभिश्चित्रमपि परार्थं संहत्य-
कारित्वात् ॥ २३ ॥

23. Though the mind has innumerable impressions and desires, it acts only to serve another, the Atman; for, being a compound substance, it cannot act independently, and for its own sake.

Every combination of individuals or forces in this world has to have a purpose for its action or existence: otherwise it would be just a meaningless, functionless collection of objects, brought together haphazardly. And this purpose must be external to itself. A congress or parliament would be just a collection of noisy individuals in a room, if it did not have the purpose of legislating for a community. A house is just pile of materials until an owner comes to inhabit and enjoy it. So with the mind — that yelling parliament of conflicting interests and desires. It is nothing but a madhouse, until it is "called to order" It can only become purposive by the external will of the Atman.

विशेषदर्शिन आत्मभाव-भावनानिवृत्तिः ॥ २४ ॥

24. The man of discrimination ceases to regard the mind as the Atman.

तदा व्रिवेकनिम्नं कैवल्यप्रागभाव चित्तम् ॥ २५ ॥

25. When the mind is bent on the practice of discrimination, it moves toward liberation.

तच्छिद्रेषु प्रत्ययान्तराणि संस्कारेभ्यः ॥ २६ ॥

26. Distractions due to past impressions may arise if the mind relaxes its discrimination, even a little.

हानमेषां क्लेशवदुक्तम् ॥ २७ ॥

27. They may be overcome in the same manner as the obstacles to enlightenment.

That is, meditation and by resolving the mind back into its primal cause (that is, attaining samadhi), as explained in chapter II, aphorisms 10 and 11.

There is a saying of Sri Ramakrishna that one needs to continue fanning oneself on hot days, but that it becomes unnecessary when the spring breeze blows. When a man attains illumination, the breeze of grace is continually felt and the fanning (the constant practice of discrimination) is no longer needed.

प्रसंख्यानेऽप्यकुसीदस्य सर्वथा विवेकख्यातेर्धर्ममेघः समाधिः ॥ २८ ॥

28. He who remains undistracted even when he is in possession of all the psychic powers, achieves, as the result of perfect discrimination, that samadhi which is called the "cloud of virtue".

ततः क्लेशकर्मनिवृत्तिः ॥ २९ ॥

29. Thence come cessation of ignorance, the cause of suffering, and freedom from the power of karma.

When a yogi cannot be turned aside from the path of discrimination even when he is faced by the terrible temptations arising from possession of the psychic powers, then knowledge is said to shower down upon him like a rain cloud, a "cloud of virtue," pouring down liberation and the bliss of God.

तदा सर्वावरणमलापेतस्य ज्ञानस्याऽनन्त्याज्ज्ञेय-
मल्पम् ॥ ३० ॥

30. Then the whole universe, with all its objects of sense-knowledge, becomes as nothing in comparison to that infinite knowledge which is free from all obstructions and impurities.

To man in his ordinary sense-consciousness, the universe seems full of secrets. There seems so infinitely much to be discovered and known. Every object is an invitation to study. He is overcome by a sense of his own ignorance. But to the illumined yogi, the universe does not seem at all mysterious. It is said that, if you know clay, you know the nature of everything that is made of clay. So, if you know the Atman, you know the nature of everything in the universe. Then, all the painstaking researches of science seem like efforts of a child to empty the ocean with a spoon.

ततः कृतार्थानां परिणामक्रमसमाप्तिर्गुणानाम् ॥ ३१ ॥

31. Then the sequence of mutations of the gunas comes to an end, for they have fulfilled their purpose.

क्षणप्रतियोगी परिणामापरान्तनिर्ग्राह्यः क्रमः ॥ ३२ ॥

32. This is the sequence of the mutations which take place at every moment, but which are only perceived at the end of a series.

The gunas, as has been said (II, 18), form this universe in order that the experiencer may experience it, and thus become liberated. When liberation is achieved, the gunas have fulfilled their purpose.

Time is a sequence of moments and, hence, a sequence of the mutations of the gunas which take place at every moment. We only become aware of these moment-changes at intervals, when a whole series of them has resulted in a mutation which is sufficiently remarkable to be apparent to our senses. For example, we are not aware, from moment to moment, that a bud is opening; but, at the end of a series, which may take several hours, we recognize the mutation, the blossoming flower. The same thing happens at the end of a series of impressions and thoughts, leading to a decision or an idea.

पुरुषार्थशून्यानां गुणानां प्रतिप्रसवः कैवल्यं
स्वरूपप्रतिष्ठा वा चित्तिशक्तेरिति ॥ ३३ ॥

33. Since the gunas no longer have any purpose to serve for the Atman, they resolve themselves into Prakriti. This is liberation. The Atman shines forth in its own pristine nature, as pure consciousness.

We shall let Swami Vivekananda have the last word: "Nature's [Prakriti's] task is done, this unselfish task which our sweet nurse, Nature, had imposed upon herself. She gently took the self-forgetting soul by the hand, as it were, and showed him all the experiences in the universe, all manifestations, bringing him higher and higher through various bodies, till his lost glory came back, and he remembered his own nature. Then the kind Mother went back the same way she came, for others who have also lost their way in the trackless desert of life. And thus is she working, without beginning and without end. And, thus, through pleasure and pain, through good and evil, the infinite river of souls is flowing into the ocean of perfection, of self-realization."

WORDS EXPLAINED AND SUBJECTS DISCUSSED IN THE TEXT